Personal and Executive Coaching

The Complete Guide for Mental Health Professionals

❖ ❖ ❖

Jeffrey Ethan Auerbach

Executive College Press • Ventura, California

Library of Congress Cataloging-in-Publication Data
Auerbach, Jeffrey Ethan.
Personal and Executive Coaching: the complete guide for mental health professionals / Jeffrey Ethan Auerbach.—1ˢᵗ ed.
p. cm.
Includes bibliographical references.

ISBN 0-9706834-0-5

1. Self-actualization (Psychology) 2. Mentoring 3. Executives—Training of. 4. Leadership—study and teaching. I. Auerbach, Jeffrey.

Library of Congress Catalog Card Number: 00-193291
First printing 2001
Second printing 2002
Third printing 2003
Author's note: The names and details of the coaching examples provided in this book have been changed when necessary to respect the confidentiality of the coaching relationships. This book is written for educational purposes only and is not intended for use as any type of psychotherapy, diagnostic instrument or legal advice.

Printed in the United States of America.

Executive College Press
3875 Telegraph Road A PMB 115
Ventura, California 93003
(805) 647-7760
http://www.executivecoachcollege.com

This book is dedicated to…

Jeanne, Micah and Ava Auerbach,
the most wonderful, loving, and inspiring wife and
children a man could dream of having

and

Louis and Fay Auerbach, my parents,
for the positive attitude, determination, and gentle
strength they modeled and passed on to me

※ ※ ※

CONTENTS

CONTENTS

CONTENTS

COACHING VIGNETTES

I would like to acknowledge my partner in life, Jeanne, for her love, commitment and care for our family while I was occupied with creating this book. I would also like to acknowledge Micah and Ava, my young children, for not creating too much havoc while I worked and for their phenomenal, bright-eyed happiness and curiosity and the motivation they give me to be the best I can be.

I would like to express tremendous gratitude to my editor, John Bergez, who calmly and extraordinarily competently took a rough draft of a book and with his encyclopedic ability to remember details from various chapters, crafted a well-flowing, easy to read volume. I also would like to thank Jeanne Woodward, my copyeditor, for her sweet spirited disposition and her willingness to speedily step in and tend so carefully to all the details necessary to producing the final text. Moreover, I would like to express my continual amazement of my design artist, Frank Boross, for his creative eye and masterful sense of style that he has incorporated into every project that I have brought him. These three individuals represent a "dream team" of a geographically dispersed group coming together with high emotional intelligence to create a wonderfully effective working relationship.

I am deeply grateful for the wonderful ideas, feedback and support of the College of Executive Coaching faculty, Ana Maria Montes, Robert Voyle, Edward Rockey, Andrea Molberg, Sylva Leduc, Relly Nadler and Sandra Foster. In addition, I want to acknowledge the tremendously important support that my peer editors, colleagues, coaches and mentors provided, Elizabeth Fellows, Marsha Markle, Jeanne Auerbach, Kristen Armstrong, Patsi Krakoff, Robert Voyle, Sharon Laurenza, Sumner Bookwalter, Ernest Rossi,

Brian Nagle, JoAnn Dahlkoetter, Paul Best, Terry Oleson, Relly Nadler and Ana Maria Montes.

Many individuals contributed examples in the form of vignettes or special additional commentary and expertise to the book, such as: Jeffrey Barnett, O. Brandt Caudill, Sylva Leduc, Bonnie Benitez, Zachary Pelchat, Mary Riemersma, Judi Craig, Paul Best, Eileen Sunzeri, Robert Voyle, Sandra Foster, Christine Brown McCarthy, Marcia Reynolds, Ana Maria Montes, Barbara Doyle, Rich Fettke, Relly Nadler, and Edward Rockey. In addition, many other individuals, unnamed here, provided useful ideas and feedback.

I also would like to acknowledge the important influence that the written works of Robert Hargrove, Frederic Hudson, Cheryl Richardson, Laura Whitworth, Warren Bennis, Peter Senge, Martin Seligman, Daniel Goleman and the Center for Creative Leadership have had on my coaching style.

PART ONE

An Invitation to Coaching

❖ ❖ ❖

CHAPTER 1

The Path from Therapist to Coach

I have written this book to help guide therapists who are interested in making the transition to the enjoyable, challenging, and satisfying work of personal and executive coaching. I have made this transition myself, and it has changed not only my psychology practice but my outlook on life as well.

Coaching focuses on helping people unleash their potential. I'm still helping people—as I did in my clinical work—but now I'm helping higher-functioning people move forward faster. My clients are extremely motivated and make progress quickly as a result of our coaching alliance.

I often work from home on the telephone. I love coaching and feel energized by my interactions with my clients. I also love helping other mental health professionals tap their strengths and help create a satisfying and lucrative coaching practice.

To help you decide whether coaching is for you, this chapter describes the path from therapist to coach. You will look at what coaching is, examine the differences between therapy and coaching, explore the characteristics of personal and executive coaching, and discover why therapists make excellent coaches. At the end of the chapter, you'll find a self-assessment to help you gauge your own readiness for coaching.

MY STORY

Let me begin by describing how I became interested in coaching and how I transformed from a therapist to a personal and executive coach.

I first began coaching after reading an article in Newsweek magazine about doing therapy over the telephone. I reasoned that therapy conducted over the telephone carried too many risks for the client and the therapist, but I began to explore types of services that a therapist could provide over the phone that would be helpful to well-functioning people and that did not raise significant ethical issues.

I began to consult with higher-functioning individuals over the telephone to help them identify their most important goals that were congruent with their key values. I followed up with weekly calls to help them stay on track. In effect, I was already on the path from therapist to coach.

At the same time I was experiencing a busy psychotherapy practice, but my practice was becoming more managed-care oriented. I no longer had people coming to me because of my particular specialty. Instead, a group of family practice physicians would blanket-refer their patients to my office because they were pleased with my services. So my practice was busy but less satisfying. It became awkward to try to refer clients that weren't a good match for me to other therapists once they already had their "authorization for service" in my name. Also, I knew that just around the corner was the prospect of being "capitated." I definitely did not want to be in the situation of being ethically and legally bound to provide whatever treatment was necessary for one very low fee.

About that time I became more involved with the psychology department of a major medical center. My colleagues had an astonishing array of high-level training from respected institutions, comprehensive experience, and a history of positions of extraordinary levels of responsibility. However, my impression was that the breadth of my colleagues' abilities was not being tapped by their day-to-day clinical work.

Then, during my tenure as chief of the psychology department, our organization was thrown into a massive reorganization as a result of a hostile takeover. During that period of crisis the mental health professionals rallied. Many of my colleagues gave their hearts, and an extensive amount of their time, to come together to brainstorm and collaborate on how best to help manage the change in a constructive manner for our clients' benefit.

Ultimately the administration of the hospital rejected the efforts of the mental health professionals. The knowledge base of organizational psychology, change management, team building, and executive development was ignored. During the ensuing two years almost two hundred mental health professionals resigned—one third of the staff. I saw my colleagues and support staff depressed and frequently in tears. The human cost of poor management affected hundreds of workers and their families.

This experience clarified for me how important it is for executives and managers to combine high emotional intelligence with inspired, effective leadership skills in order to ensure well-functioning organizations and to prevent unnecessary pain among employees. I realized how important it is for managers who lack emotional intelligence and effective management skills to get a coach to help them develop these skills. And I appreciated even more the powerful role that coaches play to help people adapt to change, create a meaningful and passionate vision of the next chapter of their personal and work life, and develop the skills to realize their vision.

Like most of you, I have always believed in a holistic approach to helping people. Now I began to see more clearly how much of our society is disenchanted with a "medical," illness-based model of health care. Yet our professions have for years been trying to appear more "medical" in the quest for insurance reimbursement. Of course, at this point insurance reimbursement and managed care have become sore points for many professionals. Not only is the "illness" model of questionable use in terms of maximizing health and recovery, but it is increasingly an outdated, unviable business model as well.

Our mutual interest in how to offer our services to the public in a manner that the public clearly values, and will gladly pay us out of pocket for, leads us naturally to the new, hot field of personal and executive coaching.

WHAT IS COACHING?

The process of coaching is similar to therapy in the sense that it draws upon many of the same qualifications and skills. But it is also distinct from therapy in important ways. The Professional and Personal Coaches Association, now the International Coach Federation, succinctly described a view of coaching that is held by most personal coaches and executive coaches:

> *Coaching is an ongoing relationship between the professional coach and the client, which focuses on the client taking action toward the realization of their vision, goals or desires. Coaching uses a process of inquiry and personal discovery to build the client's level of awareness and responsibility and provides the client with structure, support and feedback.*[1]

A similar definition of coaching is "a powerful alliance designed to forward and enhance the lifelong process of human learning, effectiveness and fulfillment."[2] Tim Gallwey, author of *The Inner Game of Tennis* (1997), describes the essence of coaching as "unlocking a person's potential to maximize their own performance. It is helping them to learn rather than teaching them."[3]

Frederic Hudson describes a coach as a "trusted role model, adviser, wise person, friend, mensch, steward, or guide—a person who works with emerging human and organizational forces to tap new energy and purpose, to shape new visions and plans, and to generate desired results."[4]

Whatever definition of coaching you incorporate into your own experience as a mental health professional, it will probably not be the type of coaching described in business books like Crane's *Heart of Coaching*, that is, management coaching with an interpersonal transformational approach.[5] The idea of managers as coaches, committed to bringing out the best in their teams, is an important one, but it pushes the boundaries set by our professional associations. Most personal and executive coaches operate from the assumption that the coach does not have authority over the client because that would be seen by many as a dual relationship. If the coach does have authority, then the opportunity for the client to develop his or her own unique agenda with the highest level of inner commitment will be limited at best, or even undermined. As a mental health professional, you will most likely develop your coaching skills to broaden your practice opportunities but not move into a management role.

DISTINCTIONS BETWEEN COACHING AND PSYCHOTHERAPY

The essential difference most often cited between psychotherapy and coaching is that psychotherapy usually focuses on resolving illness or trauma, whereas coaching focuses on enhancing achievement and fulfillment in a generally well-functioning person. Granted, some psychotherapists may have a humanistic approach that focuses on enhancing human functioning or self-actualization. But for most mental health professionals, billing insurance or managed-care companies for service by definition means certifying that they are treating an illness. Interestingly, the International Coach Federation contends that health insurance plans cannot be billed for coaching, although some companies now offer coaching to their employees as a benefit and many Employee Assistance Programs are now developing coaching services.

Professional associations and mental-health-related licensing boards will probably issue comments on the personal coaching field at some point, but at the time of this writing there are no official position papers. The American Psychological Association (APA) journal, *Consulting Psychology,* has carried many articles on executive coaching. Articles have also appeared in APA Division 42's *Independent Practitioner,* the *Psychotherapy Networker,* and other mental-health-related publications.

A dedicated group of volunteers created the International Coach Federation's *White Paper on the Nature and Scope of Coaching.* They describe coaching in a way that further distinguishes it from therapy.

This description is important for mental health professionals to be aware of, so key parts are paraphrased here with some adaptation and clarification after review from my editorial panel of mental health professional coaches. To view this document in its entire, original form, go to www.coachfederation.org.[6]

> The coaching client is someone who wants to reach one or more of the following: a higher level of performance, enhanced learning, a new level of personal development, greater career success, or increased life satisfaction. The client is not seeking emotional healing or relief from psychological pain.
>
> The coaching client takes action to move toward a goal, and often to reach higher levels of personal development, with the support of the coach. Clients who are appropriate for coaching can readily move from thoughtful reflection into action and are not significantly bogged down by "unfinished business."
>
> Coaches and clients arrange the schedule and means of contact (e.g., in person, by phone, or via e-mail) that are most appropriate to the goals of the coaching. The coach and client create the focus, format, and desired outcomes for their work. The client and the coach share responsibility for the design of the coaching agenda.
>
> Coaching is designed to help clients improve their learning, performance, and personal development and to enhance their quality of life. Coaching does not focus directly on relieving psychological pain or treating cognitive or emotional disorders.
>
> Coaching concentrates primarily on the present and future. Coaching uses information from the client's past to clarify where the client is today. Coaching does not focus on the resolution of past trauma as a precursor to help the client move forward. Thus, compared to many forms of psychotherapy, coaching spends proportionally less time discussing past upsetting events. Instead, most of the focus is on designing the future, supporting current peak performance, and nurturing the client's emerging developmental edge.
>
> Coaching assumes that there will be emotional reactions to life events

and that appropriate coaching clients are capable of expressing and handling their emotions. Coaching is not psychotherapy, and emotional healing is not the focus of coaching. Although coaching can be used concurrently with psychotherapeutic work, it is not used as a substitute for psychotherapeutic work.

Advice, opinions, or suggestions are occasionally offered in coaching. Coaches often make requests or suggestions of the client to promote action toward the client's desired outcome. Both parties understand that the client takes the ultimate responsibility for action.

The essence of why some people are interested in making a distinction between coaching and psychotherapy revolves around two issues and two camps. One camp, those who are not mental health professionals, want to ensure that there is a distinction between coaching and psychotherapy for a variety of reasons. Non-mental-health professionals do not want to be charged with practicing psychotherapy without a license. In addition, they usually have no interest in examining the past's impact on the present and future; they usually recognize that they are not trained or prepared to deal with emotional issues best treated by a psychotherapist; they know to refer clients when appropriate to licensed professionals; and they prefer to focus on vision, success, and the future.

The other camp, the mental health professionals, want to ensure that they have a way of distinguishing when it is appropriate to use a telephone-based coaching format when they may have never met the client in person. Therapists have a need for a valid and ethical method of determining which clients would be appropriate to work with solely over the telephone in contrast to in-office contact. The ethical issues of ensuring that the client receives the most appropriate service are important here, as well as the potential of liability if the coach engages in coaching when most peers would have concluded that psychotherapy was more appropriate and there is alleged harm. Generally, though, experts consider most coaching to have lower liability risk than many high-risk psychotherapy situations such as child custody issues or coping with clients with borderline personality disorder.

CHARACTERISTICS OF PERSONAL COACHING AND EXECUTIVE COACHING

The coaching process, then, has some similarities to therapy but is also a distinct type of professional work. Within the general field of coaching, there is a further distinction to be made between personal and executive coaching. Both offer opportunities to mental health professionals with the appropriate retraining.

Personal Coaching

Personal coaching involves helping generally well-functioning people create and achieve goals, maximize personal development, and navigate transitions on the path to realizing their ideal vision for the current and emerging chapters of their lives. Most personal coaching clients are focused on the development of an ideal future self, an ideal career, or an improved family life. The coach aids the client through the coaching conversation in developing a coaching agenda, incorporating values clarification, identification of strengths, and articulation of the client's current life and career purpose. The coach supports the client's efforts to engage in lifelong learning, navigate any obstacles, delegate or let go of energy-draining situations, honor challenges, and celebrate successes. Popular life coach Cheryl Richardson, author of *Take Time for Your Life*, describes her coaching as involving (1) asking provocative questions, (2) helping her clients access their own inner wisdom to guide their next action steps, (3) providing direct advice based on her experience of working with others, (4) providing focus and support to help clients keep moving forward, (5) celebrating their successes, (6) holding their hands when life gets tough, and (7) acting as a steward for the life the client wants.[7]

Helping a Client Tap Her Intuitive Strength

Jeffrey E. Auerbach, Ph.D., MPEC

A couple of years ago, a therapist colleague referred Lori to me. Lori was a 35-year-old divorced woman who was just starting out in the real estate business. She was excited about her new career and was determined to do well. Lori had been in therapy previously with the referring therapist, but the therapist felt what she wanted now was more coaching than therapy.

As I began working with Lori, I first clarified the differences between psychotherapy and coaching with her. I explained that I would refer her to a therapist if topics arose that were best addressed in a therapy setting.

We then explored her strengths, interests, and values. Next, we jointly created a coaching agenda. Lori created a personal vision early in the coaching alliance: "to live joyfully and cozily in my new home and help others do the same."

Lori was a pleasant and warm person to those she knew well, but she was not outgoing. In fact, her Myers-Briggs Type Indicator® indicated her introverted and intuitive preferences. We both wondered how she would fare in the intense sales environment of the real estate business.

Midway into the coaching process, Lori wasn't accomplishing one of the primary action goals that she had identified for herself—meeting ten new people a week. After a few weeks of her reporting her difficulty in connecting with enough new people, I borrowed one of the questions that I had developed in my therapist days. "Since we know you have a strong intuitive side," I said, "for homework this week would you like to pose this question to your wise self: How will my intuitive wisdom help me come up with a way to connect with more of my potential customers?"

I received an e-mail from Lori a few days later. "Jeff, I went for a walk on the beach and reflected on your question. I can't wait to tell you what I came up with!"

...continued on next page

> *During our next telephone coaching session, Lori said, "Do you remember how I told you I enjoy making chocolate tortes? I decided that I will spread the word via my newsletter to everyone in my territory that I'm going to be raffling off a chocolate torte every week, and that if I pick their name out of my hat, I'll come to their door and award it to them!"*
>
> *Of course, almost everyone loves chocolate, so Lori's brainstorm became a huge success. She became known as the "dessert agent" and even became something of a local celebrity. Now she had an icebreaker to make it easier to meet new people. She had developed a way to create new relationships in a manner that was fun and clever.*
>
> *This example of the pleasant and helpful interchange I often have with my clients illustrates why I find coaching so uplifting and satisfying. I enjoyed this process with Lori because it affirmed for me how my faith in the positive power of my clients' resources, along with the clients' intent to actualize their most important dreams, leads to enjoyable and rewarding work-and to powerful results for my clients.*

Often, an important aspect of personal coaching is aiding a client in transition. Coaches frequently are involved in helping people move from one phase of development to another, which parallels Erik Erikson's idea that development is a lifelong process that involves resolving successive crises.

In this connection, an understanding of Arnold van Gennep's *Rites of Passage* can be helpful to coaches.[8] Van Gennep explored how rites of passage facilitate development and transformation. He described a rite of passage as involving (1) a separation from the status quo, (2) the transition into a learning phase, and (3) the adoption of a new way of being and learning. In some ways, a rite of passage is what individuals experience when they are a member of an organization that is going through a downsizing experience or when they go through a traumatic separation such as a divorce. The coach can aid clients by framing some life experiences as rites of passage and supporting them appropriately during the transition.

In *Seasons of a Man's Life*[9] and *Seasons of a Woman's Life*,[10] Daniel Levinson explains that transitions are normal and inevitable. Since many coaching clients are going through transitions, Levinson's work is particularly relevant to coaches. Levinson describes how individuals have several developmental challenges that coaches can assist with. The five developmental components that he describes for males are forming and then modifying a dream; forming and modifying an occupation; love, marriage and family; forming mentoring relationships; and forming friendships. All of these challenges can present their own difficulties at different times in a person's life, and all are commonly discussed in coaching relationships. The fact that Levinson identifies forming mentoring relationships—which are similar to the coaching relationship—as a key element contributing to optimal development, may help explain the attraction of coaching.

In *The Handbook of Coaching*[11] and *The Adult Years: Mastering the Art of Self-Renewal*,[12] Frederic Hudson describes his view that adults experience their lives in one of two patterns: at any given time, people are either in a life chapter or in a life transition. According to Hudson, when people are in the first phase of a life chapter, they usually feel good—enthusiastic, energetic, and optimistic. Changes feel like opportunities to fulfill a life purpose. An example is a young woman just entering her career out of business school who feels challenged, energized, and excited about her future. However, when people are in the second phase of a life chapter, they feel bored and dissatisfied. Often they respond to their dissatisfaction by making a mini-transition to "tune up" their current life chapter, for example, by changing jobs (but not careers) or otherwise trying to improve what is working and change what isn't.

Less frequently, instead of entering a "mini-transition" people will enter a more profound life transition. Hudson explains that a life transition is "a transition time for starting over, while deepening the maturity of the self and its dreams." Like life chapters, life transitions consist of two phases. The first phase involves reconstructing the self, and the second includes training, experimenting, and networking. The life transition leads to a fundamentally new life direction. During a life transition people may experience feelings ranging from anger, sadness, and fear to relief and a sense of distant anticipation. This is an opportunity for deeper exploration of one's values and beliefs, which can lead to a spiritual renewal and a new sense of purpose.

In order to best address clients' needs, Hudson advocates determining which of these four phases of adult life a client is in and then tailoring coaching interventions to the unique needs of the specific life phase. For example, in phase one of a life chapter Hudson identifies assisting the client in reaching goals, taking risks, and focusing on career advancement as common coaching areas. In contrast, in phase two of a life chapter, when the client may be experiencing fear, anger, or relief, it may be more appropriate to assist the client in structuring a sabbatical, connecting with new friends, and exploring a new sense of purpose.

Transitions are often a time of soul searching. My style of coaching, which I call Holistic, Values-Based Action Coaching, rests on a foundation of the client's most important values. In this regard, I advocate incorporating a values-clarification process early into the coaching relationship to ensure that the coaching is in line with the powerful, meaningful forces operating within the client. Coaches who work with clients in transition help them clarify their personal identity, integrate a new sense of purpose, and experience increased confidence. Through coaching, clients learn to live the "being" of their life so that their actions are integrated into a sustaining pattern of their current or emerging core values and purpose.

A key characteristic of coaching is the orientation to help clients "forward their action." Rather than exploring pain or trauma, the coach helps clients maintain focus on their ideal vision of their future. So, for example, I help my clients craft a strategic life plan to give them a map to navigate to their consciously chosen future.

Executive Coaching

Executive coaching is similar in many ways to personal coaching, but it focuses especially on issues related to effectiveness and fulfillment at work. Common themes in executive coaching are developing key executive and managerial skills, enhancing teambuilding and leadership qualities, identifying and optimizing the use of key strengths, and building the competencies of emotional intelligence.

Executive coaching makes unique demands on the coaching professional. In *Behind the Closed Doors: What Really Happens in Executive Coaching,* Hall and colleagues report on the results of their interviews with seventy-five executives who were surveyed about their coaching experience.[13] Their survey led to the conclusion that the two most important factors in effective executive coaching are honest, reliable feedback and good action ideas. Twelve other qualities rated as important by the executive clients were approachability, self-knowledge, comfort around top management, intellectual horsepower, compassion, interpersonal savvy, creativity, listening, customer focus, political savvy, integrity and trust, and ability to deal with paradox.

Most of these executive clients reported that they were "very satisfied" with the coaching experience. They reported that the coaching led them to develop new skills, abilities, and perspectives, that were helpful in their careers. Moreover, the authors report that the clients experienced improvements in adaptability, identity, patience, confidence, and executive performance.

Who Can Benefit from Executive Coaching?

At this point, it's appropriate to stop and ask what an "executive" is. Peter Drucker writes in *The Effective Executive* that any knowledge worker is an executive who "by virtue of his or her position or knowledge, is responsible for a contribution that materially affects the capacity of the organization to perform and to obtain results."[14] When Drucker says "responsible for a contribution," he is implying that a key role of executives is making decisions, not just carrying out orders. Also implied is that the executive will be able to make better decisions than others because of his or her knowledge and skill.

A distinction is typically made between managers and executives. Managerial functions are often considered to be controlling, planning, and administrating. Leadership functions are usually considered to be influencing values, motives, and vision. Executives are typically required to combine these functions in day-to-day roles, but there are many managers who are not executives. Some managers may supervise many people but lack the authority to make decisions and in effect are just serving to pass on the orders and decisions of others.

Some individuals attempt to differentiate executive coaching from other forms of coaching by specifying that executive coaching means working with the most senior leaders in a large organization. However, I believe that many entrepreneurs leading small, rapidly growing start-up companies, as well as other individuals who lead complicated lives, with multiple areas of responsibility and multiple complex decision-making challenges, also benefit from working with an executive coach.

The Roles of an Executive Coach

Richard Diedrich, a senior consultant in the coaching field, has identified six major roles that executive coaches play:[15]

- Identify and modify managerial style to improve the effectiveness of individuals and teams.
- Aid the adaptation to change.
- Identify and utilize key strengths.
- Create and monitor developmental plans.
- Improve organizational performance.

- Help clients learn effective executive skills.

My research involving nineteen executive coaches from the 2000 International Coach Federation Executive Coaching Summit in Vancouver, British Columbia, sought to identify the top four executive coaching roles. I found that the four most common executive coaching roles, in order of frequency, were (1) aiding in the development of effective executive skills, (2) identifying and modifying managerial style to improve the effectiveness of individuals and teams, (3) helping executives identify and utilize key strengths, and (4) aiding in the adaptation to change.

Increasingly leaders recognize that the best way to develop leadership in their organizations is to structure challenging assignments, matched with the individual's strengths, and complement those assignments with coaching. Executive coaches can help identify strengths and explore potential areas for development through an assessment process. Then coaches create a development plan and coach the client through the plan to facilitate leadership and business success.

Executives are often faced with an overwhelming set of responsibilities, challenges, and decisions. The executive coach often serves as a strategic ally who can help executives maximize their performance by keeping them focused on their primary agendas and helping them delegate or eliminate distractions. Executive coaches facilitate conversations with their clients to help sort out the complexities in their dilemmas. Coaches serve as collaborative thinking partners and encourage the exploration of their clients' rationales, a process that can uncover errors, biases, and opportunities.

One of the most satisfying elements of executive coaching is being a part of a creative and collaborative process where extraordinary results occur. The executive coach helps to draw out creativity, innovation, and teamwork. The coach engages in this process with the executive and models a process the executive can use with his or her team. Executives need to learn how to identify and recruit exceptional contributors to their team to focus on a particular business challenge and craft a dialogue that leads to innovation. Properly trained executive coaches can help in assessing candidates for desired competencies, draw out individuals' strengths and passions to promote a best fit in the organization and facilitate maximum contribution, engage with the leader in creative collaboration, and coach the team to aid in focus, innovation, and team building.

Executive coaches can also help executives by having conversations about what leadership styles are appropriate for their situations. The coach can help executives consciously choose when, and in what combination, to

- promote an ethic of questioning
- engage in a leadership development role
- adopt a coaching and teaching role
- utilize a forceful, execution role
- foster a collaborative process
- take a hands-off approach
- focus on a supportive, encouraging role[16]

WHY THERAPISTS MAKE GREAT COACHES

One morning the faculty of the College of Executive Coaching gathered around chips and salsa at a local Mexican cantina to discuss how training in psychology and the experiences of being a therapist can help create great coaches. We identified thirteen reasons why your training and experience as a therapist gives you the foundation to be an exceptional coach:

1. Unique insights into human motivation and behavior
2. A broad perspective on the depth and breadth of human experience

3. A less judgmental interactive style than the average person

4. An understanding of people's life transitions

5. An in-depth understanding of human development

6. Experience helping people manage crises

7. The ability to balance an objective understanding of human experience with the subjective experience of others

8. An understanding of the importance of maintaining work/personal life balance

9. An ethics code that affirms the dignity of all human beings

10. An ability to help people understand that many of their thoughts and feelings are within the normal range of experience

11. An understanding of how individuals and organizations fit together

12. Training in the use of assessments to help individuals understand their personality type preferences, strengths, and areas that need extra development or management

13. Extensive experience in helping people communicate more effectively

In addition to these characteristics of therapists that would contribute to a coach's competency, our psychological literature is flush with humanistic, growth-oriented theorists who argue that healthy people can consciously choose and nurture their behavior and development[17]—ideas that provide guidance for coaches.

For example, in *The Undiscovered Self*, Carl Jung emphasized that people are motivated to develop all their capabilities.[18] He believed that our personalities continue to grow and change throughout our lives, contrary to Freud, who argued that our personalities are formed by age six. Jung asserted that our behavior is determined by our goals. In fact, Jung believed that people don't usually achieve ideal functioning until their forties as they develop and integrate all their capabilities. Jung discussed how adults often experience a spiritual awakening in the second half of life, and coaching clients are often going through this process. Also, Jung's focus on myths can inform coaches about common compelling stories in people's lives. Coaches often encourage clients to develop their own rituals to assist in a transition, an approach that mirrors Jung's interest in rituals.

D. Schultz described four characteristics of Jung's well-functioning person, which can provide guidance to us as we develop our own coaching style.[19] They are:

- a high level of self-knowledge
- an acceptance of oneself, including weaknesses as well as strengths
- an acceptance and tolerance of human nature in general
- an acceptance of the unknown and mysterious, a willingness to heed "irrational" factors without abandoning logic and reason

Victor Frankl in *Man's Search for Meaning* emphasized humans' need to make sense out of the world, to discover the meaning of the situations we find ourselves in—an idea he called the "will to meaning."[20] Coaches often are engaged in discussions about how to help people find meaning in their lives and work. Frankl's three approaches to discovering meaning can help guide coaches:

- through what we give by our creative endeavors, work or service

- through what we take from the world in the way of appreciation, such as appreciation for our spouse, children or music

- through the attitude we adopt in response to suffering

Frankl believed that ideally functioning people

- have achieved a sense of meaning in their lives
- are free to choose their course of action
- take responsibility for conduct of their lives
- are involved with something beyond themselves

Frankl's qualities of ideally functioning people parallel common coaching philosophy in that (1) clients are presumed to have their own unique answers that coaches help them discover through inquiry; (2) clients are presumed to be emotionally healthy and willing able to make choices that steer them toward their preferred future; and (3) coaching often involves a holistic, "greater purpose" dynamic.

Abraham Maslow explored what motivates behavior among people who already have their basic biological and physical safety needs met.[21] The lower level needs on Maslow's hierarchy are characterized by deficit motivation to obtain needed resources. Self-actualization, the highest level on the hierarchy, is different in that people are not trying to avoid discomfort but rather are striving to achieve a positive goal-the goal of realizing, of making actual, all of their abilities and potentials, to be all they can be.

In order to understand how people achieve self-actualization Maslow selected people who were seen by others as "fully human" and especially "alive," who had become "the best they could be." Some of the individuals, such as Abraham Lincoln, were famous, and some were unknown to the general public. Based on his research Maslow said that self-actualized people

- are realistically oriented
- are spontaneous
- are accepting of themselves and others
- have a need for privacy
- are task-centered rather than self-centered
- are autonomous and independent
- have close, intimate relationships with a few individuals
- are able to appreciate people as unique individuals rather than as stereotypes
- identify with humanity and are interested in the welfare of others.
- have (most of them) profound mystical or spiritual experiences
- do not confuse means with ends
- respect individuals from all racial and economic groups
- are creative
- have a non-hostile sense of humor
- resist conformity to their culture because they see its limitations
- transcend the environment by acting upon it rather than simply reacting to it[22]

Maslow's ideas about self-actualization can spark a wealth of coaching questions to help stimulate discussion and thought that will further our clients' development and life satisfaction. Further, his ideas provide inner guidelines for our own conception of how to help steer our clients' explorations.

Carl R. Rogers's work on how certain relationships promote good psychological functioning is fundamental to a positive coaching alliance. Rogers's three growth conditions (warmth, empathy, and genuineness) ideally underpin our coaching and personal relationships.[23] Although a few recent studies claim that these growth conditions have not proved to be consistently linked to best outcomes in psychotherapy, Rogers's ideas are central to most coaches' philosophy about creating an effective coach-client alliance.

Rogers believed that well-functioning people are open to new experiences. Although they are aware of their own feelings and attitudes, they are also aware of other elements of the world. Rogers stated that the well-functioning person "sees that not all trees are green, not all men are stern fathers, not all women are rejecting."[24] He also emphasized that individuals with high self-esteem rely upon their own personal standards instead of the approval or disapproval of others when evaluating possible courses of action. Creativity—being able to produce new, effective thoughts and actions—is another characteristic of well-functioning people. (Recently the value of creativity in business innovation is getting increased attention.) Rogers also said that fully functioning people feel free to choose between alternate courses of action. Finally, Rogers believed that a key quality of effective individuals with high self-esteem is being able to understand and accept other people as well as themselves.

These contributions of the humanistic growth theorists can help us form our own approach to personal and executive coaching, one that supports people in having conscious control of their own lives, accepting themselves with their strengths and weaknesses, using positive goals for motivation rather than just avoiding distress, and being able to change in important ways throughout their lives. Involvement in a vibrant coaching relationship taps into a person's dreams and strengths, so the coaching relationship certainly can help move a client toward Maslow's concept of self-actualization.

COACHING ORIENTATION ASSESSMENT

By now you should have a good sense of how your education, training, and experience have prepared you for the field of coaching.

To assess your initial strengths in the coaching arena and to develop a sense of areas you may want to put concerted effort into developing, rate yourself on the following items on a scale from 1 to 5, with 1 being lowest and 5 highest.

1. I believe strongly in lifelong learning.   1 2 3 4 5

2. I am effective at building personal relationships, and other people recognize this quality in me.

    1 2 3 4 5

3. I have strong "wisdom" skills that other people acknowledge.   1 2 3 4 5

4. I enjoy exploring future possibilities.   1 2 3 4 5

5. I am strong in helping others clarify action steps to move toward a goal.   1 2 3 4 5

6. I listen well without judging others.   1 2 3 4 5

7. I easily give people supportive feedback.

    1 2 3 4 5

8. I want to do something new with my skills.

    1 2 3 4 5

9. I have a strong orientation to helping people grow
    in new ways.   1 2 3 4 5

10. I can give people specific feedback about how
    their behavior is impacting negatively upon others
    or their work.   1 2 3 4 5

11. I am able to grasp the overall big picture of
    complex situations.   1 2 3 4 5

12. I enjoy helping others achieve specific results that
    they have designed.   1 2 3 4 5

13. I generously and genuinely give my ideas,
    expertise, support, and warmth to others.

    1 2 3 4 5

14. I have special knowledge or a special interest that
    suggests a unique niche coaching area.

    1 2 3 4 5

15. I am able to deliver clear and powerful messages
    that others can understand easily.   1 2 3 4 5

Review your responses to the preceding items, look for patterns in them, and ask yourself questions like these:

- What have you learned from this exercise?

- Look at the items where you chose 4's and 5's. What are a few strengths for coaching that are suggested by your responses? Generalist strengths? Specialty strengths?

- Look at the items where you chose 1's, 2's, and 3's. What are some aspects of yourself that you would like to develop further?

SUMMARY

The field of personal and executive coaching offers exciting opportunities to trained mental health professionals. Although coaching draws upon the skills and experiences of good therapists, it is distinct from psychotherapy. In general, coaching is a process of helping otherwise well-functioning people achieve key personal or professional goals—sometimes focused more on performance, sometimes focused more on developmental goals.

Personal coaching focuses on helping an individual identify and achieve important goals and often relates to individual development, balance, health, career, and life satisfaction. Often personal coaches aid clients facing a transition in their lives.

Executive coaching focuses on issues related to performance, development, and fulfillment at work. Executive coaches may be involved not only in helping individuals with issues like development of their leadership style but in coaching other areas related to enhancing personal development and the successful functioning of organizations and teams.

Historically, typical executive coaching clients have had a high level of responsibility in their organizations. However, I advocate that executive coaching need not be limited to only the most senior people in large firms. Moreover, individuals who lead complicated lives, with high-level, diverse responsibilities, may benefit from having an "executive" coach, whether or not they are executives or managers in an organization.

Therapists' education, training, experience, and personal qualities all make them excellent candidates for the role of a coach. In addition, the humanistic tradition in the psychological literature provides useful insights and guidance for coaching.

In line with our ethical guidelines of not engaging in professional work outside of areas where we have had training, experience, and supervision, an appropriate amount of retraining in coaching is required. I encourage you to assess your own readiness to transition into coaching and to identify areas of potential strength as well as areas you may want to work on developing. In the next chapter, you will take a closer look at coaching philosophy and models of coaching.

Coaching Philosophy and the CAAACS Model of Coaching

Entering the coaching field is a natural, exciting, and fulfilling step for many therapists. Coaching is a helping path that builds on therapists' communications skills and knowledge of human behavior. Coaching is especially attractive to clinicians because it provides a framework for working with high-functioning clients in a fee-for-service manner; it has a positive, non-pathological philosophy; and it is often more lucrative than clinical work.

As I discussed in Chapter 1, the move into coaching is also a transition for people accustomed to doing therapy. This chapter further explores the unique world of coaching by introducing coaching philosophy and a framework for working with high-functioning clients. Along the way I will share with you my personal style of Holistic, Values-Based Action Coaching and the CAAACS Coaching Model. At the end of the chapter I invite you to consider some of the ways in which you can continue to grow and develop as a coach.

PHILOSOPHY OF COACHING

Coaching, especially among mental-health practitioners who have transitioned into coaching, is generally practiced as a holistic process. In *Co-Active Coaching*, Laura Whitworth and her colleagues put forth a coaching philosophy featuring four elements:

- Coaching clients are naturally creative, resourceful, and whole.

- Coaching addresses the client's whole life.

- The <u>coaching agenda originates from the client.</u>
- The coaching relationship is a designed alliance.[1]

These four elements are commonly held in the personal coaching world. Although this holistic philosophy is often adhered to in executive and business coaching as well, some coaches conduct focused work that may not take the client's whole life into account.

Ultimately, both in personal and executive settings, whether holistically oriented or not, successful coaching will require the coaching agenda to be "owned" by the client to create an internal commitment to the coaching process. This idea is supported by the research of Richard Boyatzis and D. A. Kolb,[2] and others,[3] showing that people generally only learn, change, or develop when they want to.

Within this broad coaching philosophy, it is helpful to distinguish between "<u>performance coaching</u>" and "<u>transformational coaching.</u>" Performance coaching helps clients focus on fine-tuning their skills and actions, clarifying their goals, and developing action steps to help achieve short-term goals or long-term strategic plans. <u>Transformational coaching includes a process of learning whereby clients create a fundamental shift in their perspective, values, potential, and future life</u> course. Sometimes your coaching may have more of a performance flavor, and sometimes it will include a transformational quality.

The distinction between performance and transformational coaching relates to the idea that there is more than one level of learning that people experience. Chris Argyris and Donald Schon raised the idea of multiple levels of learning in executive development,[4] and Robert Hargrove elaborated on the relevance of this concept to coaching. He described what he called single-, double-, and triple-loop learning:

- Single-loop learning: Coaching people to

continuously improve their current actions or do what they are already doing better. (Incremental improvement.)

■ Double-loop learning: <u>Enabling people to fundamentally reshape their patterns of thinking</u> or practices with the intent of helping them break through impasses and expand their repertoire to approach situations differently. (<u>Learning to do different things.</u>)

■ Triple-loop learning: Empowering people to <u>alter the context out of which they make choices with the</u> intent of helping them learn, grow, and produce the results they truly desire. (<u>Transforming who people are.</u>)[5]

It is the third type of learning that leads to transformation. While single-loop and double-loop learning help people make continuous and significant progress, triple-loop learning leads to transformation of the person. Transformational coaching can take place in personal and executive coaching. In both cases, the client may be interested in making a fundamental shift in his or her life.

Hargrove describes five elements of personal transformation and "executive reinvention":

■ <u>Expand the awareness of possibilities.</u>

■ Elicit new commitments.

■ Develop a new view of who the client is—the transformational element.

■ Support new practices and ways of being.

■ Move beyond where the client was stuck.[6]

These five elements of personal transformation, the rich contribution of the major thought leaders in psychology that were covered in Chapter 1, and a command of coaching process can be internalized by the coach to form the foundation of a personal coaching style.

HOLISTIC, VALUES-BASED ACTION COACHING

I call my own style of coaching Holistic, Values-Based Action Coaching. This coaching style is holistic because the client's whole life is incorporated into the coaching agenda even though the overt focus may be related to career. It is values-based because, usually by the second coaching session, we are discussing the client's most important values, or "passion areas." This emphasis ensures that the coaching agenda rests on a foundation of what is most important to the client in his or her emerging life chapter. Finally, my style of coaching is action oriented because almost every coaching session has a focus on identifying and committing to specific actions that will move the client forward toward his or her most important goals.

Holistic, Values-Based Action Coaching clearly has performance elements because of the focus on specific actions. At the same time, it usually has transformational components as clients gain clarity about their most important goals and passions and begin to live with increased integrity in relation to their primary values.

THE CAAACS MODEL OF COACHING

In recent years, several authors have advanced coaching models: Hargrove's single-, double- and triple-loop model, Whitworth's Co-Active Model, and Hudson's Eight-Stage Model are just three of many descriptions of the coaching process. A common element in most coaching models is that coaching leads to performance improvement and in some cases may lead to a transformational experience.

To help you structure the coaching process, I have created the

CAAACS Model (pronounced "cakes"). This model organizes the coaching process into six elements:

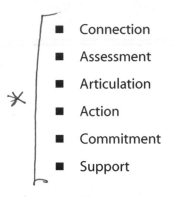

- Connection
- Assessment
- Articulation
- Action
- Commitment
- Support

Each of these elements represents a stage in both the overall coaching process and in most individual coaching sessions.

Connection

The first stage in the coaching process, both as a whole and in terms of individual coaching sessions, is to connect with the client. When you connect with clients, you are establishing rapport and gaining an understanding of their perspective, thoughts, and feelings.

To test whether you're connecting with a client, you may ask yourself questions like these:

- Where is the client's focus? Is the client genuinely focused on the conversation, or is he or she preoccupied, ambivalent, or untrusting?
- Is there unfinished business troubling the client that must be addressed?
- Have I cultivated an interest in the client's strengths and successes?

Once you have determined the client's focus, communicated interest and support for his or her current situation, and determined that no major distraction is blocking your client from focusing on moving ahead with the coaching, you are ready to move to the next stage, assessment. However, sometimes the first stage of connection and the second stage of assessment are necessarily intertwined, or partially reversed. When any unfinished business is so pronounced that adequate focus on the coaching agenda is affected, you may want to ask clients if they want to talk about that challenge for part of the session "to clear their mind" or if they prefer to compartmentalize that business and set it aside so that you can focus on the next step.

Assessment

The second stage of coaching involves conducting an assessment of the client's current situation, strengths, areas of development, values, and goals. Through this process the gap between where the client is and where he or she wants to be becomes more evident.

Several types of online assessments or paper-and-pencil assessments can be used in this stage. A new-client questionnaire enables you to gather information quickly about a client's career and personal life and provides a snapshot of the individual's goals and aspirations. You may develop your own questionnaire for new clients or use the one provided in the Appendix. You will gather further information during the initial interview, discussed in Chapter 4. In addition, you may want to make use of assessments such as the Myers-Briggs Type Indicator to help clients understand their dominant personality style and preferences, enabling them to have greater awareness and an easier time choosing behaviors and options that best fit various challenging situations. Most importantly, assessments also aid you in choosing what style to use in working with clients to best aid them in the coaching process.

Articulation

Once you have a general understanding of clients' particular situations, the next step is to help them articulate the desired focus of the coaching. Here you help clients challenge themselves to reach higher and to articulate their dreams and goals.

Articulation begins with a process of visioning in which you aid clients to envision a preferred future. To do this, you may use visualization or other methods to help clients get in touch with their dreams, declare their passions, and vividly imagine their ideal life or their ideal of success.

Having clients share some of their peak experiences in the first couple of sessions is a good way to set the stage for the realistic use of vision in coaching. When clients acknowledge peak performance or past accomplishments, they lay the foundation on which they can later build plans to achieve their most compelling vision. Further, your helping clients uncover and identify their strengths sets the course for coaching on a positive tack rather than on a course that can increase feelings of self-doubt.

To help clients identify their strengths, you can ask them in a homework inquiry to identify:

- periods of rapid learning
- qualities of excellence they possess
- extended periods of high performance
- what is particularly satisfying to them
- what they yearn for

Next, you engage in "focusing"—a directed conversation to lead clients to establish the major areas of the coaching. Initially you may ask the client, "What do you want to focus on (or accomplish) in our coaching work together?" While you may verbally contract with the client to work on the desired focus area, often it is most effective to work together with the client to draw up a written coaching plan (also called an agenda or development plan). The agenda establishes the general goals of the coaching. In subsequent sessions, you will usually have a "focus" discussion with your client to articulate and agree on the purpose of the day's session. That is, you will reflect back to the client something to the effect of, "So today our focus will be . . . Is that right? If so, tell me more about where you want to go with this."

As the client articulates the focus of a coaching session, it is important to ask yourself, "How does this focus area fit with the client's central values and the emerging coaching agenda?" If the focus of the discussion seems to be straying from the emerging core coaching agenda, you can point out the digression and help the client return to the major focus or consciously choose a different direction. You might say, for example, "This sounds like an important topic but one that is beyond our original coaching agenda. Is this area of sufficient importance to you that you want us to expand the coaching agenda? If so, can you first say more about how this challenge fits with your most important values?"

It is important not to shortchange this process of exploration and articulation. Early in the coaching relationship you are engaged in a process of helping your client share goals, problems, challenges, and opportunities. New coaches, hearing that coaching involves forwarding the action, sometimes rush into planning before enough exploration or clarifying is accomplished. The danger is that plans are concocted or decisions are made that may not match the client's values or realities.

Therapists are usually skilled at drawing people out. It is most helpful to adopt a conversational style that conveys that you are interested in your client's perceptions, ideas, and dreams and that you recognize that your client is smart and sophisticated. Avoid an attitude of deep, troubled concern that you might display when exploring a painful experience in psychotherapy. Responses such as these will be helpful:

- "That's interesting ... Tell me more."

- "That sounds like a great idea because it fits with ... Tell me more about that."

- "What do you think about ...?"

- "Can you give me an example about how that plays out?"

Through these kinds of responses, you reflect your clients' thoughts. Next, it's important to notice and comment on the congruency of these thoughts with the clients' stated values and goals. If you are skilled in metaphor, you can use metaphors to help clients know they are understood.

Part of the task in facilitating articulation is to help clients discover whether any part of their thinking is limiting them or blinding them. Increasing the clients' awareness of any "blindspots" they have is a principal value of coaching. If their thinking is distorted or limited, you can help them explore the rationale for their thinking and acknowledge any unintended consequences. Then you help them adopt more realistic and accurate thought processes. Here you can borrow from cognitive therapy, and utilize your reframing skills, to increase their possibilities for personal and professional growth by helping them adopt accurate, rational thinking.

This exploring and clarifying component of the articulation stage can be transformative, as some clients will begin to see themselves, and their potential, expand. As clients create a clearer understanding of themselves and their thought processes, they will feel more focused, confident, and inspired. This empowerment prepares them to formulate, and execute, challenging plans.

Action

After assisting clients in declaring their dreams, vision, and mission in the articulation stage, you next help them convert their vision and dreams into challenging but attainable goals, to validate these goals in terms of their stated values, to commit to action steps that will move them forward, and to successfully complete these steps.

At the outset of the action stage, you serve as a confidant for clients to bounce ideas off of as well as a provider of honest feedback to help clients adopt goals that are challenging, congruent with their values, and realistic. You then guide them through the process of building action steps, with a timeline, to support their goals. Action in this case could be external action or the intention to reflect on an inquiry.

The process of translating goals into actions has three elements, all of which you facilitate as a coach: (1) brainstorming potential relevant actions, (2) considering the pros and cons of each action and selecting the best, most useful action, and (3) aiding in anticipating obstacles and preparing a plan to manage them.

An important factor to remember is that the actions must be sufficiently challenging so that some movement occurs, but not so challenging that they are not accomplished. Here are some questions that might guide your thinking and questioning during the action stage:

- What does the client want to be different?
- What does the client want to do more of?
- What are the client's strengths and resources in this area?
- How will the client move forward?
- How would the client like it to be?
- What may get in the way?
- What is the client's plan to manage each challenge or obstacle?

The secret for successful fulfillment of the action stage is, as much as possible, to let the clients identify and choose the actions to be taken and lead in the action planning. Generally clients are better equipped to identify what they need to do in the coming week than the coach. However, with some clients who may be slower to identify what they need to do each week but nevertheless show great commitment to their vision and the coaching process, I have found that carefully crafted direct suggestions of challenges and actions can also be highly effective.

Commitment

Once clients have begun to develop action steps, it's time to focus on commitment. In the commitment stage, clients are specifically committing to the date, time, and place of engaging in the "homework" actions they brainstormed in the challenge stage.

The process of encouraging your clients to first identify their passion, values, and mission enables them to have high internal commitment to the work they are doing with you on their self-selected goals. Clients are usually ready to commit to a specific action plan when they have generated their own ideas, challenges, and solutions; addressed obstacles that may arise; and feel support and encouragement from you.

You provide support and accountability by facilitating your client in making the commitment; asking the client to contact you on a specific date with a progress report; providing realistic, honest feedback; and encouraging the client to enlist the aid of others in achieving his or her goal.

As a coach, this is when you ask, "What are you planning to do specifically, when are you planning on doing it, and how will I know how you are coming along with that goal before our next session?" Clients might respond, "I'll send you an e-mail before our next appointment to tell you what progress I'm making."

This commitment to themselves, and to you, automatically creates an accountability that is fundamental to achieving positive outcomes in coaching. Clients are much more likely to accomplish a goal if they have made a commitment with you to accomplish a specific task by a specified time and date.

Support

Your role in the support stage is to provide encouragement and help clients identify and cultivate other supportive people and factors in their lives that increase the likelihood of their success. With adequate support, clients' self-confidence will increase, as will their resourcefulness in utilizing their current skills, expanding their skills, and trying out new ways of thinking and acting. The right amount of support will enable clients not only to "hang in there" when things get tough but to achieve breakthrough performance and reach developmental milestones. The importance of support and practical steps to achieve it are discussed further in Chapter 11.

Exercise Using the CAAACS Model

Here is an exercise in using the CAAACS Model. A registered nurse calls you and says she wants to leave nursing. She wants to work with you on a new career path. She has two teenage children, ages fourteen and seventeen. She is married. She likes to exercise and is involved moderately with her church. She is not sure of a new career path, but she knows that she wants to be able to work part-time.

Using the CAAACS Model of Coaching, how would you proceed? What are some of the coaching questions that would be appropriate in the different stages of the model? What are some of the coaching conversations that would be useful for your client?

The Coach as a "Talking Mirror"

Sylva Leduc, M.Ed., MPEC

A number of years ago I was working in an organization that was experiencing low morale. Staff members had expressed their dissatisfaction with the style of management of their department's executive director—and this was not a quiet or shy group! They were so vocal that they had gone to the VP of their department and complained bitterly. When I first met with the executive director, he explained he'd tried many different management techniques, including having an open door policy, but still people were unhappy and he couldn't understand why.

As we were talking his brow furrowed, he became demonstrative and began wagging his finger at me quite emphatically. I experienced an immediate visceral reaction. Thinking that I might have stumbled upon one of the keys to the employees' dissatisfaction, I made the following comment: "I've just had a curious feeling that I want to tell you about. Do you remember when you were little and an adult would reprimand you by shaking his or her finger and saying, 'No, no, don't do that'? Well that's sort of how I feel now. I'm feeling as though I'm being chastised for something I've done wrong. Let's explore my reaction and see if it's anything similar to what your employees experience."

We then had a lengthy discussion of the impact of nonverbal communication and about how people will believe the nonverbal messages over what's being said when there appears to be an incongruity in communication. Over the next few weeks my client monitored his nonverbal messages. In one of our following coaching sessions he proudly reported that staff were commenting on how much more accessible and approachable he'd become. Within a short period of time he'd made some rather remarkable progress. When I asked him what he thought was the reason, he

...continued on next page

smiled, winked, and confided, "Now when people come into my office, I sit on my hands."

This is a humorous example of the power of responding in the moment, showing how valuable honest feedback is for a client and how the coach can be a "talking mirror" for discussing what occurs in the organization.

THE IMPORTANCE OF PERSONAL MASTERY AND DEVELOPMENT

So far I've discussed the philosophy of coaching and model of the coaching process. But there is another major piece to the puzzle: the continuing development of the coach.

Outstanding coaches, like outstanding therapists, undergo a lifetime of learning and personal growth. Outstanding coaches are effective because of who they are, combined with appropriate technique. Communicating masterfully is connected to personal development as much as to technique. Ideally, professional coaches actively pursue lifelong learning by reading, attending conferences, and engaging in formal training opportunities.

Your Self-Perception

Part of your personal development as a coach involves examining how you see yourself in the coaching role. As you think about coaching, or periodically as you coach, you may want to take a good look at your view of yourself.

Your self-perception may evolve from how you saw yourself as a therapist. For example, you may adopt a new view of yourself as coach that includes

- seeing yourself as a person who has an impact on people's vision, values, and sense of future

- identifying yourself more as a growth facilitator than a therapist dealing with negative or problematic behavior, less as someone who heals pain and illness and more as a professional who aids high-functioning people clarify and achieve goals and maximize their personal development

Adding Business Language to Your Communication Style

Since many of your coaching clients may come from business and corporate settings—especially if you make executive coaching your specialty—you will probably need to upgrade your vocabulary. Much coaching is conducted in organizations where the common vernacular may include terms like ROI (return on investment), knowledge management, scalability, and mission, vision, and values. Even if your clients don't come from large corporate settings, it is likely that many of them will be entrepreneurs. Subscribing to the *Wall Street Journal, Fast Company, Fortune, Harvard Business Review,* or *Business Week* is a practical way to upgrade your vocabulary so that you can share a common language with your business-oriented clients.

Here are some examples of themes, terminology, and concepts you may want to become familiar with:

- benchmarking
- best practices
- change agent
- competitive advantage
- continuous improvement
- corporate culture
- downsizing
- e-commerce

- human capital
- intellectual capital
- Kaizen
- knowledge management
- line items
- mission, vision, values
- outsourcing
- performance management
- process improvement
- product life cycle
- rightsizing
- ROI (return on investment)
- scalability
- six sigma
- speed to market
- supply chain
- team building
- upstream and downstream
- mastermind groups
- value added
- value proposition

SUMMARY

Transitioning into the coaching field is an attractive, natural step for many mental health professionals. Compared to the crowded field of psychotherapy, there are relatively few well-trained personal or executive coaches—especially with graduate degrees.

Philosophically, coaching emphasizes a positive, humanistic perspective. Coaching clients are seen as capable and resourceful. Most coaches value working with a holistic perspective and believe the client has primary responsibility for creating the coaching agenda. Some coaching centers more on performance (improving clients' skills or success in particular areas), while other coaching has a transformational element (helping clients to reach new levels of personal development, and thereby gain new perspectives on themselves and their world). Regardless of the focus of coaching, the process is most effective when the client has high internal commitment. To build commitment, coaches strive to ensure that the coaching agenda is primarily designed by the client.

I call my style Holistic, Values-Based Action Coaching because (1) the person's whole life is incorporated into the coaching agenda, (2) exploration of the client's values ensures that the coaching agenda rests on a foundation of what is most valued by the client, and (3) most coaching sessions focus on practical steps to either improve performance or enhance personal development.

There are a number of models of the coaching process. The CAAACS ("cakes") model includes the six elements of connection, assessment, articulation, action steps, commitment, and support. These elements describe stages of the coaching process as a whole, as well as the flow of many individual coaching sessions.

At this point you have an overview of coaching as a professional opportunity, coaching philosophy, and coaching process. The next chapter explores legal and ethical issues that are specific to the coaching field.

Ethical and Legal Issues in Coaching

CHAPTER 3

As you know, anyone can call himself or herself a coach; no licensure is required. I believe the fact that many of you reading this book hold a mental health license is good for the consumer. Your familiarity with the laws and ethical concerns that you have incorporated as a mental health professional will motivate you to conduct yourself with the highest ethical principles in mind.

Fortunately, because the type of coaching described in this book involves working with high-functioning people and does not involve the high-risk areas that are generally associated with behavioral health lawsuits, the risk of liability claims is regarded to be much lower than when conducting therapy. However, there still are liability risks, such as if a coach is accused of giving poor business advice.

If you have both a coaching practice and a clinical practice, you will want to maintain a distinction between the two. If you are doing telephone-based coaching, you will want to have a set of guidelines to clarify which types of clients are appropriate for telephone-based coaching versus which types of clients your professional peers would conclude would be better cared for through in-office psychotherapy.

The state in which you are licensed, and whether your background is psychology, marriage and family therapy, or social work, may make a difference in how you describe yourself and how distinct you want to make your coaching practice from your licensure. For example, if you are a psychologist, you may be seen as operating under the scope of your licensure, whereas if you are a marriage and family therapist, your legal counsel may advise you to keep your coaching completely separate from your licensed clinical practice. In either case, experts agree that you will want to make it clear, verbally and in writing, that you are providing coaching services, not psychotherapy.

The legal and ethical issues in this emerging field contain gray areas and unanswered questions. Licensing boards and professional associations have issued few guidelines. Moreover, licensing regulations vary from state to state, further clouding the ability to provide any specific answers. Fortunately, these gray areas are not deterring mental health professionals from moving into this emerging field. I believe this is positive, as our professional development prepares us to be leaders in the coaching field, and we have the ability to bring the benefits of positive psychology to the greater public.

In this chapter, numerous ethical and legal issues will be raised and explored. I will report to you the results of many conversations I have had with the legal counsel of professional organizations and with clinicians around the country. You will also have the benefit of contributions from Jeffrey E. Barnett, Psy.D., past president of the Maryland Psychological Association, and O. Brandt Caudill, Jr., Esq., both of whom publish extensively on legal and ethical issues.[1] You will also find the observations of Bonnie R. Benitez, Esq., and Zachary Pelchat, Esq., both legal counsel for the California Association of Marriage and Family Therapists.[2] Keep in mind, however, that I am not an attorney, and I cannot give you legal advice. Wherever possible, I have included the perspective of leading legal and ethics advisors in the mental health field. However, this material is presented for informational purposes only, and you must consult with your own ethics committees, licensing boards, and legal counsel on any specific questions you have.

MAINTAINING THE BOUNDARIES BETWEEN COACHING AND CLINICAL PRACTICE

Generally, it is important to keep clear boundaries between psychotherapy and coaching. From an ethical and legal point of view, the line between therapy and coaching is often defined by whether a mental disorder is present and the percentage of time that the coach or therapist focuses on healing pain or trauma.

The Impact of Your Licensure on Your Coaching

Coaching, as it is generally understood, does not require a license, and there is no organized effort to implement a licensing requirement. Training programs like the College of Executive Coaching's Master Personal and Executive Coach Certification, which requires a graduate degree, are addressing the need for mental health professionals to obtain appropriate training and experience as they move into a new area of practice.

If you are a licensed psychologist, personal and executive coaching is usually considered within the scope of your licensure assuming that you have specific training and experience in this area. Attorney O. Brandt Caudill comments: "The broader a state's license law defines the practice of psychology, the greater the risk that someone could argue that coaching falls under it and requires a license. One of the broadest such definitions is in California (BPC Section 2902)."[3]

Many psychologists who have transitioned to coaching maintain very clear distinctions between psychotherapy and coaching, especially if they are doing telephone-based work. I think maintaining this clear distinction is advisable. At times, however, the line between coaching and therapy may blur for the psychologist. If you are working in your office, for example, you may feel prepared, as well as qualified by your license, to assist people to navigate through painful emotions if they arise in the coaching session. Moreover, as a licensed psychologist conducting coaching in your office, you may be very willing to incorporate a deeper level of work into your coaching—work that might sound like psychotherapy to most of your peers. For example, you might help clients explore their fears or pain and then use coaching techniques to design a path forward.

The complication here is, what are you really doing, psychotherapy or coaching? What expectations does the client have of you? How does your written agreement characterize the work you are doing together? Chapter 4 further explores the initial coaching process and the importance of having written and verbal agreements about the scope of coaching.

In contrast to the above example, let's say you have a telephone-based coaching practice. You are not face to face in the office. Here you must maintain an even firmer line between coaching and doing therapy. For example, I believe it would be inappropriate to engage in a type of coaching over the telephone that is going to frequently encourage the client to move into painful or fearful areas without your being physically present. O. Brandt Caudill comments: "Psychologists should be aware of the American Psychological Association's (APA) position statement on telephone therapy, because they are held to knowledge of such statements as APA members. Non-APA members should review the position statement to be aware of the APA's view, since some state license boards use APA standards for disciplinary purposes."[4] (An excerpt of the APA statement can be found in the Appendix.)

Of course, strong emotions will occasionally arise in sessions conducted over the telephone, and when that happens you will do your best to assist your client. Well-functioning clients would be expected to have occasional emotionally upsetting events that they want to talk about in coaching, but their basic emotional wellness indicates that they are unlikely to be harmed by your not being physically present as they discuss these issues over the telephone. For example, say that you were engaged in telephone-based coaching with a well-functioning client (that is, one with no mental disorder) and the individual began discussing his fears of rejection and the pain of previous rejections. In telephone-based coaching, you would be oriented to listen to the client express those feelings, usually in a relatively brief time period, and then conjointly design action steps to move forward, whereas in therapy you often would spend more time and energy exploring the pain and connecting it to other painful experiences in an effort to heal previous unresolved pain.

On the other hand, it would be inappropriate to engage in telephone-based coaching with a client who has a mental disorder, spending considerable time exploring the person's emotional pain. Most of your peers would conclude that you could provide considerably more assistance, and care for your client better, by being physically present, because it would be reasonable to predict that your client is likely to be emotionally distraught often.

Jeffrey Barnett adds: "It seems very important that each licensed mental health professional be aware of the relevant laws in the jurisdictions in which they are practicing. It is possible that some licensure boards will rule that a psychologist, for example, is using his or her training in psychology to do coaching or that the individual is actually practicing psychology regardless of what one calls it. Therefore, it is important that each of us knows local laws and perhaps writes our local licensure board for a written ruling on the practice of coaching by licensed mental health professionals."[5]

If you are a marriage and family therapist or a clinical social worker, your license may not clearly be interpreted to include coaching with non-mentally ill clients. Does this mean that MFTs should not engage in coaching? Absolutely not! Like other mental health professionals, you have skills that can be transferred into the coaching realm. However, Bonnie R. Benitez and Zachary Pelchat, counsels for the California Association of Marriage and Family Therapists, recommend that you make a sharp distinction between your coaching practice and your psychotherapy practice. The previous discussion may help you understand and adapt to the ethical issues.[6]

Perhaps because of the great efforts that marriage and family therapists have placed on winning equity in the reimbursement markets, the emphasis in the language of some states' licensing laws has become focused on treating mental illness. However, I think this focus and possibly overly narrow perspective on scope of practice are misplaced. Clearly practitioners of marriage and family therapy, social work, and psychology can, with appropriate training, offer much to the coaching field. In fact, one could argue that the orientation to systems that many mental health professionals have presents a special, valuable focus that can naturally be adapted to a coaching model.

A related issue is the use of coaching techniques outside coaching proper. Although this application is outside the scope of this book, all therapists can benefit from familiarity with the coaching techniques described here. Many clinicians report that coaching techniques are easily adapted to working with clients with mental illness, providing a refreshing, positive, behavioral, and outcome-oriented focus. Even using the old, narrow definition of marriage and family therapists as solely concerned with relationships, family, and children, it is easy to conceive of many families and relationships where there is no presence of a mental disorder but there is great interest in creating a higher quality of life—exactly the focus of many personal coaches. Furthermore, the scope of practice for marriage and family therapists is now broadly considered to include the treatment of almost any mental disorder, as long as there is an important relationship component and the practitioner has the appropriate training and experience. I see nothing in the licensing law that suggests that marriage and family therapists, social workers, or psychologists are precluded from assisting well-functioning people with coaching techniques that most observers would report have similarities to humanistically oriented cognitive-behavioral approaches.

In the states where licensing laws apply, social workers often have a more broadly written licensing law than that of marriage and family therapists. Social-work licensing laws generally include a reference to enhancing organizations' effectiveness, which is also the role of many executive coaches. Hence social work, given the philosophy of many of the training programs, has parallels to the field of coaching.

Certainly, there are some similarities and overlap between coaching and other professions, such as mental health, consulting, and training. Still, coaching is emerging as its own profession, with its own ethical guidelines and professional associations (the International Coach Federation and the Professional Coaches and Mentors Association).[7] In general, the field of coaching is in the pioneer stage, and although associations in the helping professions are beginning to offer courses in coaching at their annual meetings, there are few official positions that have been taken regarding coaching. My hope is that the behavioral health care professions will continue to embrace the coaching field while encouraging appropriate retraining in coaching so that we move away from a disease model to a positive, strength-based coaching model.

Literature Providing a Basis for Coaching by Mental Health Practitioners

Organized psychology already has an extensive literature base devoted to executive coaching in the American Psychological Association journal *Consulting Psychology*. Many articles on personal coaching have appeared in the *Independent Practitioner*.[8] Recently the *Psychotherapy Networker* and the *Family Therapy News* have run several pieces related to coaching. I expect to see more literature on coaching from all the mental health fields in the next few years.

THE NEED FOR A MENTAL HEALTH SCREENING

A primary question for mental health professionals is how to determine whether a client is an appropriate coaching client. In particular, the coach should attempt, within the practical means of the coaching relationship, to ascertain whether the client has a mental illness. If a mental illness is suspected, offering a referral to a licensed mental health professional is warranted. Whether to offer coaching if the client currently receives mental health treatment from another licensed mental health professional is a question that needs to be examined on an individual basis.

The primary challenge is how to be reasonably assured that a client is appropriate for coaching, especially if your only contact with the client is over the telephone. A second challenge is how to explore this question when the client is contacting you overtly for coaching with no awareness that this is a concern of yours. How do you explore these issues with a new client without creating awkwardness for you or your client?

I have found that there are four steps. What follows is a more cautious approach than many coaches with mental health training follow, but it does offer you a guideline to consider.

1. In the initial telephone conversation, clarify that your style of coaching does not include any type of counseling or therapy for any type of mental illness. Also clarify that generally coaching has proved very helpful for your clients but that it is possible that someone might experience some changes that might bring some difficulty for the client. You might say, "For example, you might conclude to resign from your job at some point and then have a period of struggle while you search for a good fit. I cannot promise you any particular result except to do my best as your coach to help you reach toward your highest goals while maintaining your values and vision."

2. In your written agreement, specify that you are not providing any type of psychotherapy or treatment for mental illness and that you would make a referral to a licensed mental health professional if such issues arose.

Ethically and legally you are, of course, required, as with all clients, to have a written agreement about the nature of your work together, including possible risks and benefits. O. Brandt Caudill comments: "A written agreement is a practical necessity, although it may not be required by state law. Coaching agreements should never be referred to as informed consents, because informed consent applies generally to patients. Also, remember that in referring clients to therapists, you must actually know something about their qualifications or you could be sued for negligent referral if they act negligently."[9]

3. In your initial session, clarify with your client that although

you are trained in psychotherapy, you are not providing psychotherapy in this coaching relationship.

4. At this time—and this is the step that many coaches do not take, especially in executive coaching relationships—also review and clarify briefly with the client the results of your assessments and ask a few important mental health screening questions to help you decide if your client is more appropriate for coaching or psychotherapy. An example of a screening question is "Has there been a time in your life when things got so bad that you felt like trying to end it all?" In other words, a two-pronged approach of written assessments and verbal discussion is useful in conducting a simple screening for the possibility of a mental disorder and in helping to determine the appropriateness of coaching versus psychotherapy.

If a client seeks coaching with a coach who has both a therapy practice and a coaching practice, and if the coach determines that therapy would be more appropriate than coaching, some legal counsel has recommended that the coach should refer the client to a different licensed or certified mental health professional. In these circumstances bringing the client into your own practice might be construed as a dual relationship.

Jeffrey Barnett adds: "I would also strongly recommend that in the agreement/contract there be a statement the clients sign saying that they will notify you immediately if any mental health difficulties arise during the course of the coaching relationship so you may make an appropriate referral. Such a statement puts some of the burden on them to notify you rather than having it all on your shoulders."[10]

Overall, you want to have a documented process of how you determine whether a particular client is appropriate to work with in a coaching relationship or whether you, and likely your professional peers, would conclude that it would be more appropriate for the client to be served through in-office psychotherapy. When someone does warrant a referral for mental health treatment, document your thinking and actions, and make the referral.

When you make a procedure like this to protect yourself and your clients, follow through on it. The time therapists are likely to get in trouble is when they deviate from a well thought-out protective process because they are "just trying to help."

CONFIDENTIALITY

Ethical standards also require you to clarify for clients that you intend to keep your coaching relationship with them confidential. You should explain orally and in writing that there are limits to confidentiality as well as exceptions to confidentiality that are required by law.

You should also clarify in writing that the notion of "privilege" may not apply in coaching. For example, if for some reason you were required to testify in court and you were maintaining that you were doing coaching, not psychotherapy, then the idea of privileged communication would probably not apply and you would be required to testify. Coaches who hold a mental health license are required to meet the legal requirements of mandated reporting even if they claim that they are not operating under their psychotherapy-related license. However, when they do argue that they are not operating under their psychotherapy license, then it would follow that they cannot argue that their records are "privileged" from subpoenas. Again, the important point is to apprise your client of your intention to maintain confidentiality while making clear the limits of confidentiality. Discussing your intention to maintain the confidentiality of your conversations will also help build trust and openness.

Marriage and family therapist specialist attorneys such as Bonnie Benitez and Zachary Pelchat have stated that since coaching is unregulated, MFTs should understand that coaching does not fall under the license and that coaching conversations are not privileged.[11] In other words, you may have the ethic to maintain confidentiality, but the conversation is not legally "privileged" in the sense that it is not necessary for there to be a court order for you to share information about the conversation.

MAINTAINING PROFESSIONAL BOUNDARIES

Professional boundaries need to be maintained with coaching clients. However, coaches may notice some differences between the boundaries with their coaching clients compared to the boundaries they have with clients that are in therapy. Boundaries with coaching clients often feel a little more relaxed than those with therapy clients, because coaching clients are generally emotionally healthy and less fragile than most psychotherapy clients. Also, by the nature of the coaching agreement, you may be required to travel to meetings or attend working meals with coaching clients—situations that rarely arise with therapy clients. You should evaluate the appropriateness of the boundaries that you maintain with your coaching clients on a case-by-case basis. If you have questions on a particular situation, you are advised to consult with your ethics committee.

VIRTUE ETHICS

Jeffrey Barnett argues that mental health professionals benefit from having an internal set of "virtues" that help them sort out whether or not particular situations are ethical.[12] This idea of having a mental set to evaluate how to handle situations is especially helpful in emerging areas of practice where there are not clear standards set by the professional associations. Here are some questions to ask yourself as you coach in order to foster this kind of mental set.

- Are you acting with *beneficence*—the virtue of helping others and acting in the other's best interests?

- Are you operating with *no malfeasance*? That is, are you reasonably sure you are not doing any harm?

- Are you conducting yourself with *fidelity*, being

faithful to your obligations and agreements with your clients?

- Are you conducting yourself with *veracity* by being truthful and honest in all your endeavors?

- Do you have the virtue of *high self-care?* Because coaches are often in the position of being a role model to others, appropriate attention to our own self-care enhances our attractiveness as coaches, ensures that our profession is not tarnished by unprofessional conduct, and helps us to maintain sound judgment and behavior.

Barnett further advocates that we ask ourselves these questions to evaluate our interactions with our clients:

- Will my client be helped by this action?

- What negative events might happen from this action?

- Am I acting in accordance with our agreements?

- Am I deceiving my client or anyone else by acting in this way?

- Am I encouraging independence or dependence in my clients?

- What would my coaching colleagues think of my actions?

- Confidentiality aside, would I be comfortable having other coaches reading my notes?

RECORD KEEPING

In clinical work, when you write a note during your session, it can be distracting and anxiety-producing for you and your client. In telephone-based coaching, you can make notes without distracting your client. Take advantage of this by keeping notes of your coaching sessions to aid you in tracking your client's goals, challenges, and actions. If you are a mental health professional, most states require you to keep records of your sessions. Often, not keeping records of your sessions is tantamount to negligence.

Jeffrey Barnett stresses the importance of documentation: "Effective documentation is an important risk management strategy. Not only have courts ruled that if it isn't documented, it didn't happen, but they have also held that an incomplete or inadequate record is an indication in itself of the quality of services provided."[13]

Even if you maintain that your coaching sessions are not psychotherapy, in the event of a legal proceeding the opposing attorney could argue that you were engaged in psychotherapy. Your defense would include your notes, which would illustrate what you were and were not doing in your sessions. Remember that when you are engaged in coaching, as opposed to psychotherapy, your records may not be protected by privilege and easily be subpoenaed.

I recommend that you use a preprinted form to help you organize your coaching session notes. My coaching form includes the client's name, overall session number, session number in the current payment cycle (for example, session 2 of four paid sessions), past actions, challenges, goals, action plans, client comments, and coach's thoughts. A sample coaching notes form is included in the Appendix.

OTHER ETHICAL ISSUES: QUESTIONS AND ANSWERS

In our training programs, which are conducted around the world, I hear many common questions from mental health professionals who are attempting to reconcile the guidelines they operate under given their mental health licenses and certifications with the unlicensed and unregulated coaching role they are transitioning into. Here are some frequent questions and the answers commonly given by the attorneys representing mental health professionals. (Again, keep in mind that the author is not an attorney and does not provide legal advice. Mental health professionals are best advised to operate with the highest possible standards and to consult with their mental health ethical committees and legal counsel when complex issues arise. This material is presented for informational purposes only, and you must verify with your own legal counsel how it may apply to your specific situation.)

Q: Can I coach a friend?

A: The answer may depend on what you mean by "coach." Early in their training, it is common for coaches to ask a friend to help them "practice some of the coaching techniques I'm learning in my training program." So this is a common approach used to gain experience and can easily fit into how people ideally nurture their friends and help them move toward their dreams.

However, most coaches would find it uncomfortable to have a true professional coaching relationship with a close friend, billing the friend at the relatively high rates that coaches charge. Furthermore, would you be able to give a friend or family member the same quality of useful, honest feedback on their counterproductive patterns as you would an independent client? The idea is that one role can impair the effectiveness of the other.

Because coaches may often receive requests from friends to coach them, an ideal arrangement is to have a coach colleague to whom you can refer your friends and at the same time to develop relationships with other coaches who will refer their friends to you. In that way you will be filling your practice with paying coaching clients, rather than spending considerable time coaching friends gratis.

Q: Suppose I have just received a large coaching contract from a firm, and I greatly need the income. What do I do if the company CEO says, "Tell me about the details of the coaching discussions with my employees"?

A: You can tell the CEO, "In my professional experience the only way I have found to provide maximum value to the companies that hire me is to assure the employees I am coaching that I will strictly maintain the confidentiality of the material they tell me to the extent the law allows. I will communicate to you whether the client is attending the coaching sessions and whether I believe the sessions are helpful to the client. I'd ask that you trust my professional judgment in what it is important for me to communicate to you or the Human Resources Manager."

Jeffrey Barnett adds the following point: "I would be sure to have a contract with all clients, whether they be individuals or corporations, that details all the issues mentioned earlier, including the limits of confidentiality. Prevention is the best risk management approach. It is also a great business approach. The only surprises you want your clients to have is how wonderfully they've been helped by you. You don't want to hear such things as 'But I need to know that' or 'I thought everything was confidential.' This is just as you would do with fees. You clarify what you charge, what services you provide and don't provide, and how you are to be compensated. All this is best addressed and agreed to verbally and in writing up front."[14, 15]

Q: Should I put my mental health license number on my business cards?

A: Jeffrey Barnett answers, "It is very important for all mental health professionals to not use their specific mental health credentials in advertising their coaching services. Putting the license number on the cards brings with it a number of implications. The average consumer would have greater difficulty keeping the two roles of psychotherapy and coaching separate. Since you're not doing psychotherapy, why put your license number on your card, invoices, letterhead, or advertising? Keep the roles separate. You can put your name, highest degree, and your professional title or role, such as 'Executive and Personal Coaching.' This makes it much more clear what you are doing professionally."[16]

Similarly, Bonnie Benitez and Zachary Pelchat, counsel of the California Association of Marriage and Family Therapists, argue that MFTs should leave their license numbers off their cards so they don't imply to the client that when they are doing coaching they are also operating as marriage and family therapists.[17]

Q: I'm trying to keep my coaching practice separate from my clinical practice. Should I list my mental health background and licensure or certification on my brochure or website?

A: Perhaps, because your qualifications can bolster your credibility. I would definitely list your graduate degree. I think your advanced training and license or certifications represent that other professionals have independently affirmed that you have advanced skills and knowledge. Many people who engage in coaching have no advanced degrees or special training in psychology, interpersonal dynamics, or the helping fields. In fact, many coaches with no advanced degrees are eagerly seeking a coaching certificate in part so they have some "initials" to put after their name because they feel sensitive that they don't have enough "credentials."

The reason it may be appropriate to list your mental health license in your biography, but not on your cards, is that in your biography you have the luxury of describing how your background increases your competency while you also have the space to clarify what your current coaching services do and do not include. Of course, you need to be thoughtful in how you present your background so it doesn't confuse the professional coaching image you are presenting or the service you are providing. For example, if your goal is to increase your CEO leadership development clientele, then emphasizing your past clinical duties in a psychiatric hospital would detract from your image, while mentioning your past management of a National Institute of Health research project would build credibility.

Q: Either over the telephone, or by commuting across state lines, can I coach someone in a different state than the one in which I am licensed?

A: The most conservative, lowest-risk approach would be to operate only in the states in which you are licensed. However, in the consulting field, many consultants who also are licensed mental health professionals operate across state lines and conduct consulting businesses like training or team building in states where they do not hold a license without suffering legal consequences. In clarification, though, they are not practicing psychotherapy. This area of using new technology like teleconferencing is one that the professional associations have been researching, but as of this date they have not issued an official position on it.[18]

Q: In my written agreement with my clients, should I specify that I am a mandated reporter, that is, that there are specific situations where I legally must break confidentiality and make a report?

A: Yes.

Q: May I have past therapy clients in my coaching practice?

A: This question must be examined on a case-by-case basis. Many people refer to the "two-year rule," whereby, in many states, it would be unethical to have sexual relations with a client until at least two years have passed. Clearly, it would be safer never to have sex with a former client. The same could be said about coaching. It is a continuum of risk and safety. It could be argued that the more time that has passed since the conclusion of therapy, the less risk there is of abusing any type of power dynamic. Many therapists will be able to point to their therapy practice as having been largely cognitive-behavioral, focusing on humanistic, goal-oriented agendas, not significant mental illness, and they will argue that although they will look at every client individually, there is not a risk of harm to clients if they accept them as coaching clients.

Again, if you believe that you have a questionable case, or if you believe your professional peers would view the situation as harmful or risky, seek a consultation with your professional association's ethics committee. Your priority has to be on making reasonably sure that your client will not be harmed.

Q: Are there confidentiality risks in using mobile phones, cordless phones, and e-mail? May I use them in coaching?

A: The reality is that many clients use these types of technology regularly. It could be argued that to ensure the strictest confidentiality a regular hard-wired phone would be preferred. However, in my experience, many coaches and clients prefer the flexibility of cordless phones, mobile phones, and e-mail even though they know there may be some risk of decreased assurance of confidentiality. In fact, because of many wireless long distance package plans, many clients now prefer to make all their long-distance calls with their wireless, mobile phones. In addition, technological advances have made wireless technology more secure than it was a number of years ago. For example, the manufacturers of "spread spectrum" cordless telephones assert that they are generally secure from eavesdropping.

Jeffrey Barnett adds: "The use of technology should be included in the agreement, and the coaching client should be informed of the risks to confidentiality of using certain media, such as the Internet and cordless phones. It is then their choice. If they decide to send e-mails, for example, and request you do so as well, then you are doing so with their permission."

SUMMARY

Coaching provides many new practice opportunities for mental health professionals but enters into areas where the ethical and legal guidelines are only beginning to be clarified. As always, it is your professional responsibility to consult with your professional peers and ethics committees, and to obtain appropriate legal counsel, when you have particular ethical and legal questions.

Generally, you will want to maintain a distinction between your coaching practice and your clinical practice. To make sure that your client is receiving the most appropriate service, you should operate under a set of guidelines to clarify which types of clients are appropriate for coaching versus which types your professional peers would conclude would be better cared for through in-office psychotherapy. If you determine that a prospective client would be better served with psychotherapy, then refer the individual to an appropriately licensed or certified mental health practitioner.

Although there are no firm, official guidelines regarding coaching from the mental health professional associations at the time of this publication, there are a variety of suggestions coming from leaders in the respective fields depending on whether your background is that of a psychologist, marriage and family therapist, or social worker. For example, psychologist licensing boards may consider that coaching falls under the psychologist's licensure, although they will usually see coaching as distinct from psychotherapy. Marriage and Family Therapy professional associations may recognize that your professional training will enhance your ability to be an effective coach, but they recommend keeping your coaching practice separate from your clinical practice so your clients will be clear about whether they are enrolled in coaching or psychotherapy.

In order to determine whether a prospective client is appropriate for coaching, many clinicians-turned-coaches are utilizing a client questionnaire, assessments, and a series of screening questions. If you judge a client to be more appropriate for psychotherapy (for example, because of the presence of a mental disorder, or because the client's goals are primarily about healing emotional pain rather than moving forward with important personal or career goals), then you should make a referral to an appropriate mental health professional. If you have both a therapy practice and a coaching practice, and you determine that a client who approaches you for coaching would be better served through therapy, you should refer the client to a different licensed or certified mental health professional rather than bringing the client into your own practice, which might be construed as a dual relationship. In all cases, you should document your assessment and thought process in determining whether clients are appropriate for your coaching practice.

Always advise clients that you intend to keep your coaching conversations confidential, but also apprise them of the limits of confidentiality, including mandated reporting as required by law. In addition, apprise the client that since this is a coaching relationship, not a counseling relationship, "privilege" may not apply. In other words, your records probably would have to be turned over to a court if subpoenaed.

As with therapy, you should maintain professional boundaries with your clients, but you may find that these boundaries are somewhat more relaxed in the case of coaching. If you have questions about a particular situation, consult your ethics committee.

Jeffrey Barnett's concept of virtue ethics may help you develop a mental set of continually evaluating coaching situations from an ethical point of view. Among the questions to ask yourself are whether you are operating with beneficence, with no malfeasance, with fidelity, with veracity, and with proper attention to self-care.

As a coach, you have a professional responsibility to keep adequate notes about your coaching sessions. Keep in mind that such notes may easily be subpoenaed in the event of a court action.

The legal and ethical issues in this emerging field include some gray areas and unanswered questions. Licensing boards and professional associations have issued few guidelines related to coaching. In this chapter, issues were explored in terms of the most recent information; hopefully, new information and clarifications will soon become available.

I am not an attorney, and I cannot give you legal advice. The material in this chapter is presented for informational purposes only, and you must consult with your own ethics committee and legal counsel on any specific questions you have.

PART TWO

Coaching Process and Techniques

❖ ❖ ❖

CHAPTER
4

Initial Process

As in most professional relationships, coaching has a beginning, a middle, and usually an end. The beginning of the coaching relationship includes establishing rapport, creating trust, assessing personality type and interpersonal style, and identifying and clarifying the coaching agenda. The middle phase of coaching usually includes coaching conversations about challenges, strengths, values, passions, strategic career-and-life planning, inner challenges and outer obstacles. This phase also includes the use of accountability to further the actions of the client. The latter phases of the coaching relationship include validating progress, coaching emerging goals, preparing to conclude coaching, arranging follow-up coaching, and possibly a good-bye letter or celebration.

This chapter discusses the opening phase of coaching, that is, what to accomplish in the initial process—from the first contact through the development of the coaching agenda—and some tips for how to go about it. Although coaching is a client-centered process that requires you to respond to every client's situation in a unique manner, the following discussion of the early contacts with a new client will aid the newcomer to coaching.

INITIAL TELEPHONE CONTACT

In this section I introduce you to parts of the actual dialogue you may have with a prospective client. Much of this discussion relates to an inquiry for personal coaching. Later in this section I'll comment on how this process is adapted for executive coaching in an organizational setting.

In my initial telephone conversation with a potential client, I explain the structure of the coaching relationship—the number of sessions I normally schedule with a client per month, the length of the sessions, and the fees—as well as answer other questions the client may have about the relationship.

With these basic steps in mind, here are some tips about handling the initial call from a prospective client. Begin by warmly greeting the caller, and then clarify how he or she came to be referred to you. Inquire as to what brings the caller to contact you for coaching at this time. After listening to the response, verbally reflect your understanding of why the person is seeking coaching. For example, if you sense the possibility of a greater potential for the caller, and if it seems appropriate to do so, you can share your perception:

> *"I sense that you want to create much more in your life [job, career, etc.] and that coaching can help cross that divide between where you are now and where you want to be."*

Assuming the caller expresses interest in taking the next step, explain how you work with people and add that coaching often focuses on clarifying clients' own ideal visions for their lives. Explain that it is usually goal- and action-oriented and is not a form of psychotherapy or treatment for emotional pain or disorder. (I like to refer to the relationship as the coaching "alliance" representing a joint commitment between client and coach.) At this point, you might say something like the following:

> *"You may know that I am also trained as a psychologist, but I like to make it clear that our coaching relationship is not a psychotherapeutic relationship, which often focuses on problems or on mental illness, but rather an alliance focused on accomplishing your goals and creating your version of an ideal life or an ideal career. Coaching focuses on future*

possibilities and how to turn them into reality. If issues arise that are best addressed by in-office visits with a psychotherapist, I will refer you to a licensed psychotherapist."

If the conversation is moving toward the client hiring you, clarify your fees, confidentiality policy, and services. If the client is ready to begin coaching, explain what you will be sending before the first session—an agreement, a new-client questionnaire, and perhaps a web link to your online assessments (see the Appendix for sample forms). Request that the client mail you a check for the first month's coaching fees or provide you with credit card information at the first session. If you are doing predominantly telephone-based coaching, request a photograph "so that I can put a face with your voice." Your client may already have an image of you from your brochure or website; if not, send your picture to the client. Agree on at least the first appointment time (I usually schedule the first four appointments).

When a new client promptly receives the agreement and questionnaire that the coach promised to send, it further increases confidence that the coach is reliable and trustworthy. Moreover, the establishment of a clear, written agreement promotes trust and comfort because the agreement answers basic questions about the coaching process.

The assessments that I have the client complete are usually the new-client questionnaire, the Myers-Briggs Type Indicator®, the FIRO-B® (Fundamental Interpersonal Relations Orientation-B®), an adjective checklist, sometimes the California Psychological Inventory®, and sometimes an emotional intelligence assessment. (A detailed discussion of assessment is in Chapter 7, and a discussion of emotional intelligence is in Chapter 10). For speed, the College of Executive Coaching uses online assessments that comply with test manufacturers' procedures and American Psychological Standards. Online assessments also avoid the ethical problem of mailing sensitive testing material, which could jeopardize test security.

In an organizational setting, the initial call inquiring about executive coaching often comes from a Human Resources professional about one or several of their employees. There, the initial process may be different. If possible, I still try to arrange a phone call with each coaching client before the first session in order to have a variation of the discussion just described. This telephone call can help to reduce anxiety for the employee, answer any preliminary questions, enable you and your client to get a "feel" for each other, and build interest and enthusiasm for coaching. When dealing with an organization, a contract or letter of agreement is usually completed with Human Resources or a particular executive. The payment details and confidentiality information are specified in that agreement.

PREPARATION FOR THE FIRST COACHING SESSION

Before the initial coaching session occurs, you usually have in hand the new-client questionnaire, some assessments such as the Myers-Briggs Type Indicator®, and perhaps an adjective rating scale such as the Profile of Mood States. You also have your notes of what you have heard from the client in the initial phone call or notes from the referral source, such as Human Resources.

Carefully review the information you have received. (I usually read through the new-client questionnaire twice.) Clarify for yourself, and document in your notes, that based on the available information, the client is appropriate for coaching and that your professionally trained peers would not conclude that the client would be best served in an in-office, psychotherapeutic setting for the treatment of a mental disorder. Of course, if it became clear from the initial assessments that coaching was not appropriate at this time, you would have a conversation with the client about appropriate resources or referrals and refund any money already provided.

FIRST COACHING SESSION

Welcome the client to the session. Thank the client for returning the questionnaire and agreement, completing the assessments, and sending the check for the first month's coaching (often three or four sessions), or, if need be, gather the client's credit card billing information. Explain more about your approach to coaching, and explain that you will be designing the coaching alliance together. For example, you might say:

> *"I believe the best coaching occurs when the coach and the client design the relationship together. Let's talk about the structure of how we will work together to accomplish your goals ..."*

Explain that you have reviewed the new-client questionnaire but that you have found it helpful to begin by having clients tell you in their own words more about why they are seeking coaching at this time and what they are hoping to get from the coaching relationship. Continue to ask questions to help you clarify key forces in the client's life by focusing or elaborating on the questions in the new-client questionnaire. Here are some examples of questions and prompts that are appropriate at this time:

- "What brings you to coaching now?"
- "Tell me more about what you are hoping to get from the coaching relationship."
- "What do you want to focus on in the next three to six months?"
- "Tell me about a time in your life when you felt particularly energized and focused—a period of high performance or satisfaction. What was going on and who was involved?"
- "What are your career goals?"

✗ ▪ "What would be important for me to know about your family and personal life?"

In addition to clarifying whether coaching is appropriate, these initial questions will help you begin to establish a connection with your client on a deeper level. When you ask, "What brings you to coaching now?" you learn about the client's motivation and desires. When you ask, "What would be important for me to know about your family and personal life?" you learn about the client's support system and often about other critical joys and challenges. For example, this open-ended question might lead you to learn that your client has a seriously ill family member, went through a bitter divorce, or has just reached five years of sobriety. When you ask, "Tell me about a time when you felt particularly energized and focused," you are learning about a strength that sets a positive tone for the first coaching session.

Clarifying Your Agreements with the Client

Creating clear agreements with new clients builds trust. In this connection, during the first session it's important to clarify what will be included in the coaching and what is outside the coaching relationship. For example, the client should understand that your role as a coach includes asking many questions and taking on other facilitative roles, but does not include counseling or psychotherapy. You should also make clear to your clients that the effectiveness of coaching depends on their following through on the commitments they make to themselves. Let them know that what moves them forward are the actions they take, and that you cannot perform those actions for them. By the end of the first coaching session your clients should understand that you intend to help them with their unique coaching agenda. This might include helping them to focus; maximizing their personal development, for example, by building emotional intelligence competencies; providing an accountability process; and providing support and encouragement as well as confronting the client when he or she strays from the course.

Discussing your intention to maintain the confidentiality of your conversations also helps to build trust and openness. As discussed in Chapter 3, however, you should also explain that there are some exceptions to confidentiality that are ethically and sometimes legally required of you.

Clarifying That Coaching, Rather Than Psychotherapy, Is Appropriate

Verifying that a client is a suitable candidate for coaching, as opposed to psychotherapy, is one of the reasons for the assessments that you send after the initial telephone contact. Recall from Chapter 3, however, that it's wise to combine written assessments with some discussion. The first session is the time to have this conversation. (This discussion is most appropriate on occasions when a mental health professional coach is conducting telephone-based personal coaching. Most executive coaches do not verbally inquire about mental illness history or therapeutic treatment, because the executive coaching relationship is more clearly circumscribed than the newer subfield of personal coaching.)

After reviewing the written assessment material, conduct a conversation with your client to clarify that he or she is appropriate for coaching as opposed to psychotherapy. Keep in mind that the client is overtly seeking coaching, not therapy, so you need to be tactful and clear about why you are asking these questions. Here are some things you might say to broach this issue:

- "Since I have been trained and licensed as a psychologist (counselor, psychotherapist, marriage and family therapist, or social worker), it is ethically important for me to ask you a few questions to clarify whether coaching is appropriate."

- "I'd like to ask you a few questions that help clarify the best approach."

- "Are you interested in focusing on particular areas of your career or your life in general, developing plans of action, and moving forward with your plans in between our appointments?"

- "In your background have there been times when you felt particularly down or depressed? If so, can you tell me about them?"

- "Is there any history of mental illness in your family?"

- "Have you had any type of therapy in the past? How about currently?" (Note that many coaching clients will answer yes to having had therapy in the past.)

- "Are you taking any type of medication for depression or anxiety?"

- "Have things ever gotten so bad that you tried to end it all?"

- "Have you found substance abuse to be any kind of issue in your life? Have other people told you that they think it is?"

This conversation can sometimes feel awkward because the client is not bringing anything up about depression and suicide, and here you are taking time to talk about this in the first session. My experience is that if you explain why you are asking these questions, people understand and respect the reason for them. You can ask these questions in a professional and sincere manner that doesn't bring extraordinary attention to them. Don't apologize too much for asking or make a bigger deal about this than it is.

If you learn information in the first session that leads you to conclude that the client has an emotional difficulty best treated in a context of therapy, make the referral, document the process in your notes, and refund the first month's payment (since the client is not receiving the service he or she contracted with you for). In my experience, however, this is a rare occurrence. Clients who need psychotherapy generally seek psychotherapy, and clients who are appropriate for coaching seek coaching. In addition, clients who need therapy will usually contact someone practicing psychotherapy so that they can bill their insurance for the service, whereas coaching is not reimbursable by insurance. Moreover, in those instances where someone does seek coaching inappropriately, most often you will have identified the mismatch before the first session, either in the initial phone contact or by reviewing the assessments returned by the client.

It is possible, although extremely unusual, to inadvertently enter into a coaching relationship with a person who has a borderline personality disorder. Because of the complexities of dealing with this type of client, immediately seek an ethics consultation with your peers or professional association to determine the best approach to managing the referral process. This possibility, although remote, necessitates that you do not let the distinction between coaching and psychotherapy become fuzzy. Furthermore, this example highlights the importance of having verbal and written agreements clarifying the scope of coaching and indicating that you refer appropriately to other professionals when issues arise that are best treated in a psychotherapeutic context.

CREATING A COACHING AGENDA

In addition to establishing trust and rapport, in the initial coaching sessions you and the client conjointly begin to clarify the focus of the coaching agenda.

The creation of the coaching plan or agenda is a multifaceted process that guides the coaching relationship. The agenda must be client centered and client generated, because it must be backed by the client's internal commitment to be effective. If it is the spouse's agenda or the employer's agenda, the client's internal commitment will likely not be sufficient to pull the client significantly forward.

Clients usually have an agenda, or purpose, in mind when they call you for coaching. They may have heard that you coach entrepreneurs and they want to get their business more organized and double their income, they may be executives who have been referred to you to achieve a developmental goal to enhance leadership, or they may have heard that you are a spiritual coach and they want your help to create a life of greater joy and balance. During the early sessions, you begin with the client's agenda and then work with the client to design the coaching alliance with the aid of the new-client questionnaire, assessment, values clarification, the Life Focus Satisfaction Scale, and coaching conversations.

Establishing the Focus of Coaching

Early in the relationship, aid clients to determine their initial focus. The first three questions in the New-Client Questionnaire in the Appendix ("What do you want to be sure to get from the coaching relationship?" "How do you want me to be as your coach?" and "What do you want to work on in coaching?") can be used to launch the initial discussion of the coaching agenda. Additional questions related to challenges in career or in life and the focused question "What do you need to change to move forward?" will give your conversation specific focus. Questions and prompts such as "What do you believe in strongly?" and "Tell me more about your personal and family life" will introduce the idea of values and a holistic perspective to the coaching relationship.

Conducting a values-clarification process early in the coaching relationship is useful. Do the initial areas of focus fit with the client's values? Is there sufficient space and time in the client's life to develop the identified coaching areas? If not, then the client may first need to simplify his or her life by entering into a coaching relationship to support delegating or letting go of energy-draining situations.

Some clients will excel in identifying specific goals and work in an intensely focused manner to achieve their stated purpose. Others will identify general areas they want to work in and will make gradual and intermittent progress. There is no one right way to go. As a result of the variety of human personality, motivation, and preferences, both ends of the spectrum (and the points in between) are to be expected, valued, and supported in coaching.

Clarifying the Goals of Executive Coaching

In executive coaching, co-designing the agenda includes deciding with the client the specific goal to be achieved. Executive coach and consultant Robert Witherspoon has outlined the four roles that executive coaches are frequently called upon to play. Witherspoon explains these four roles in his Coaching Continuum Model:

- Coaching for skills: focusing on a client's current project or task

- Coaching for performance: focusing on a client's effectiveness in a present job

- Coaching for development: focusing on a client's future job responsibilities or career or both

- Coaching for an executive's agenda: focusing on a client's larger issues, including better business results[1]

Initiating a discussion about which of these four roles the client seeks will help guide you in the type of goals to establish and help you estimate expected time frames and fees. Finally, it will help you determine the most applicable assessment process and measure outcomes. Although as a coach you may play several different roles during your work with a client, to avoid confusion about expectations it is best to identify a primary role.

Coaching for Skills

Coaching for skills focuses on a specific task or project. A skill can be a method, strategy, or behavior that would correspond with success on a particular project. The time frame of coaching for skills often is relatively brief: one session, one week, or one month.

As an example of coaching for skills, an executive sought help to sharpen her speaking skills for a major presentation that she was to give in two weeks. The coaching consisted of three appointments in the two-week time frame. The first session consisted of sitting together and brainstorming ideas the executive felt were important to cover and helping her identify a humorous story she could begin with. The second and third coaching sessions took place in a large room. These sessions focused on helping the executive eliminate abstract material and add more inspirational stories from her team. The coach provided feedback on the timing of her stories, modeled ways to increase the dynamic nature of her voice, and helped her become comfortable with the microphone and ready to respond to impromptu questions.

Coaching for Performance

Coaching for performance helps people improve in the current context of their career or personal life. This type of coaching may take place over many months.

For example, a manager came to coaching because he was dissatisfied with his performance in motivating his team to meet sales goals. The coach initiated an assessment process whereby multi-rater feedback assessments were given to the manager and his supervisor, peers, and direct reports to obtain feedback on the manager's motivational style. The coach assembled the assessments into a report and reviewed them with the manager in a half-day coaching meeting. The coach and client then developed a coaching plan to help the manager improve his motivational approach with his team. Coaching was conducted in person and over the phone for six months, and the team's production increased twenty percent.

Coaching for Development

Coaching for development focuses on where the client wants to go in the future. This type of coaching is often used to help clients develop competencies that will facilitate a promotion or new career opportunities. Coaching for development may last nine months or longer.

One client, for example, needed to develop ways to overcome some weakness in her managerial style. She consistently received feedback that she appeared too indecisive to others, yet she was a star in other areas and could be eligible for a major promotion. The coach gave the client assessments (a multi-rater feedback assessment, the FIRO-B®, and the Myers-Briggs Type Indicator®) and reviewed them with her. Over several months coach and client together explored the client's ideas regarding decision making. The coach also observed the manager in meetings and used a systematic feedback style to help her develop a more decisive style. During the eight months of coaching, the sessions tapered off from every week for the first three months to every other week by the end of the process. After one year the client had been promoted. The coaching was credited with facilitating the promotion by generating observable changes in her decision-making style.

Coaching for the Executive's Agenda

Coaching for the executive's agenda often focuses on the larger issues in the leader's life. The leader of a complex business, or the individual leading a complex life, often benefits from having a confidant—someone to bounce ideas off, explore different ideas and perspectives with, get constructive feedback from, and explore visionary ideas and strategy with. Many executives relate to the phrase "It's lonely at the top" because of the difficulty they have confiding some of their concerns to the people under them. The confidential relationship with a professional coach is often a welcome opportunity to discuss a variety of business, personal, or strategic issues that for one reason or another they may not want to share with others. This type of coaching may go on for several years, often beginning with regular meetings and over time becoming more flexible.

As an example of coaching for the executive's agenda, one executive was seeking a change in his career and lifestyle. The executive sought a coach to help him develop a long-range strategy to move from a successful executive career into a consulting relationship with his company in two years. The coach conducted assessment sessions and engaged in a coaching dialogue with the executive, including several joint sessions with the executive and the executive's spouse. Since one of the client's goals was to create a more fulfilling chapter of life with his spouse, his wife was involved for the additional perspective she offered, feedback on the desirability of contemplated key steps, and the joint visioning process. The coach helped the executive develop a clear vision of what he wanted the next chapter of his life to be like and helped him craft an appropriate consulting career model. Then the coach helped the client prepare for a successful succession for the position he was leaving by grooming a member of his staff for promotion with whom he had a strong working relationship. The coaching lasted approximately two years and resulted in a win-win situation in that the company was able to retain the competitive advantage of the executive's expertise, while the executive client was able to adopt a more flexible lifestyle to match the personal vision that he and his spouse had created.

Helping an Executive Client Achieve Her Work/Life Goals

Judi Craig, Ph.D., MCC

A director-level executive in a large (five-billion-dollar) Midwest retail organization requested coaching for two issues: (1) she had great ideas, but couldn't sell them (particularly to senior executives) and (2) she was working an eighty-plus-hour week with resulting issues around work/life balance.

This was a person who was highly respected and admired by her direct reports and staff, yet the senior management team was not promoting her. Through coaching, she began to be more visible to the senior group by implementing the following strategies:

- informing her superiors via written memos on the status of various projects she was heading up (she was contributing a lot, but how would they know?)

- livening up her presentations with the use of humorous stories and cartoons (to counter her "serious, calm presentation style")

- risking speaking up in meetings when she had a contribution (previously, she would let opportunities pass because she felt she had to have all her points thoroughly thought out before she spoke)

She accepted my request to limit her office time to fifty-five hours per week, a significant reduction. To do so, she allocated her travel (which she did two to three times a month) to Tuesdays; if she did not have to travel, she scheduled nothing in order to have a day to "catch up." She would break this standard only if her CEO requested a meeting. She batched her phone calls and left paperwork and administrative details to the last two hours of the day, when her energy level was lowest.

...continued on next page

She also negotiated with her husband to have every Wednesday night as "their night." Both avoided doing any household chores or work left over from their workday and instead used the evening for planned activities they both enjoyed. The couple also decided to plan a one-day outing one weekend day a month (or overnight, when possible).

To complete the life-balance issue, one piece was missing: she did nothing for herself! She loved sketching and oil painting, but she hadn't picked up a paintbrush in over six years. In addition to learning to nurture herself in brief "time-outs" during the day (sipping a cup of tea, watering her plants, brushing her cat, doing "fun" reading), she scheduled one Sunday a month (in advance!) to sketch and paint.

Interestingly, this executive received an impromptu call from her boss about two months later. He said, "I see you've been leaving around 5:30 instead of working late and that you're not coming in weekends anymore." Fearing a lecture, she admitted this was true. "I wish you'd tell me your secret," he continued, "because you're so much more productive now!"

A month later she was promoted to vice-president.

Designing a Coaching Agenda Based on Mutual Trust

The creation of the agenda is the culmination of the initial process of coaching. It may take one session or several to define the coaching agenda. The keys are to ensure that the agenda is one that the client owns and is committed to and that the agenda is achievable in the agreed-upon time frame.

Co-designing the agenda further establishes a relationship based on trust and mutual respect. In coaching, the Rogerian dynamics of genuineness, empathetic listening, and positive regard will help clients feel that you are their ally. Having a history of credibility; having integrity; providing relevant, useful advice; and making it clear that you will give your client realistic feedback—all help set the stage for collaborative agenda design. When a client perceives you as genuine, trustworthy, and competent, an environment of safety is developed that facilitates the discussion of the client's biggest challenges and most important dreams.

SUMMARY

This chapter has emphasized the opening stages of the coaching relationship. Coaching requires a client-centered approach, in which each client's unique values, goals, and often dreams are incorporated into the coaching process.

In the initial contact with the client, explain the structure of the coaching relationship (for example, whether you will meet in person or on the phone), the scope of coaching compared with other types of professional services, and the fees. Discuss the nature of the coaching relationship, and put it in writing. Provide the client with assessments, which will serve as a basis for the coaching agenda. Review the assessments in preparation for the first coaching session.

In the first session, clarify your agreements with the client. At this time you should also engage in a conversation to help ensure that the client is appropriate for coaching versus another professional service such as psychotherapy.

In the early sessions, focus with your client on clarifying the goals of the coaching relationship and co-designing a coaching agenda to which the client will have high internal commitment. It is helpful to come to an understanding with the client on whether the coaching will focus primarily on skills, performance, development, or a combination of areas that fit the client's needs.

Building trust and mutual respect early in the relationship will help create a powerful coaching alliance. Coaching competencies such as genuineness, sincere interest in the client, credibility, and the ability to provide relevant, useful feedback will create a coaching climate of collaboration and commitment.

chapter 5

Developing the Coaching Alliance

Development of the coaching alliance rests on the creation of mutual trust and respect. Several factors help clients begin to develop a constructive coaching relationship with you, beginning with the initial process steps discussed in the last chapter. As the relationship develops, demonstrating your interest and commitment to your clients' goals and their welfare helps clients know that you are supportive of their success. Promptness and consistency— following through on what you say you will do—help to convey your integrity and sincerity. Having maturity in your own awareness of your feelings, being able to maintain an overview of the process while engaged in conversation, and having a good sense of when to share intuitive insights all strengthen your ability to create an alliance with a new client.

In addition, in the early sessions both the coach and the client can get a clearer sense of what they are expecting from each other, and they each can give feedback on their perception of the realism of these expectations. At this stage, your ability to be highly interactive with your client, your use of humor when appropriate, your ease of adaptability to your client's interests, and your ability to draw out from your client the most important areas to focus on in coaching all help to continue building trust and a powerful working relationship.

Your early interactions with the client set the stage for a mutually designed alliance in which you and your client have equal power. The Ready for Coaching form and the New-Client Questionnaire (see the Appendix) will help you create a setting that emphasizes clients' willingness to make a commitment to the coaching process and their responsibility for setting the agenda and determining the direction of the coaching. Incorporating the results of assessments such as the Myers-Briggs Type Indicator® will aid you in developing a strong coaching alliance by helping you adapt your communication and questioning style to the preferences of each client.

UNDERSTANDING AND WORKING WITH THE CLIENT'S WORLD VIEW

Building relationships of trust with clients includes learning about their perceptions, world views, and learning styles, respecting their concerns, and communicating in a manner that fits with each client's personality type, life experience, and learning orientation. In *Coaching: Evoking Excellence in Others*, James Flaherty emphasizes the importance of understanding that a client's interpretation of events is a factor of the client's observations, background, and mindset.[1] He refers to a story told by Frederick Perls about three individuals who attend the same party. Each of the three guests has a different view of the evening. The first guest is an artist who examines the art on the walls. The second guest is an alcoholic who looks for the booze. The third guest has a crush on the hostess and only has eyes for her. Although all three people attend the same party, their perceptions and memories of the event are quite distinct.[2]

As a coach, it's important for you to understand how different individuals can interpret and behave differently in the same environment. Through skillful questioning, you can help clients reveal and explain their thought processes—what data they are focusing on and what conclusions they are drawing. You then choose the particular words and attitudes to focus attention on previously ignored areas. You thereby facilitate a new interpretation of situations as the client comes to realize the possibility of broader perspectives and alternative perceptions.

The language engaged in by coaches is one of the building blocks of a unique relationship. For example, introducing the importance of the values underlying life plans early in the coaching process helps to establish a relationship that has substantial depth, as opposed to a surface discussion of "plans." When you craft a coaching conversation in important areas for a client, the language of the discussion then becomes integrated into the client's vocabulary. In this way, the introduction and exploration of specific concepts provides a model to enable client self-regulation when the coaching relationship has concluded.

DEVELOPING TRUST IN SHORT TIME FRAMES

To develop trust quickly, especially in a telephone-based relationship, where the client cannot see the sincerity in your eyes, you must convey that you are a trustworthy professional with your voice and your actions. Trust is built gradually based on your actions. Here are some tips for building trust quickly:

- Fulfill all commitments. Don't promise something unless you will do it promptly.

- Be on time to the calls.

- Send material that you say you are going to send.

- Maintain a high level of professionalism in your actions and comments (i.e., promptness, maintaining appropriate boundaries, thoughtful and respectful replies).

- Establish a clear, respectful, and nonjudgmental communication style.

- Communicate with empathy and reflect key ideas back to clients so they can trust that you understand them.

- Create an environment of safety, openness, and confidentiality.

- Maintain frequent contact with clients to build a sense that you are "there" and trustworthy, for example, by sending an email response promptly when a client sends you a homework assignment.

- Trust that your clients will follow through on what they say they are going to do. When they don't follow through, bring the matter up with them in a straightforward manner. For example, "How would you like me to respond when you don't do something you said you would do?"

- Trust that clients can accomplish what they say they can.

In executive coaching, when you enter into a new coaching relationship with an organization, consider the following suggested steps to develop trust, rapport, and an appreciation for the company culture:

- Clearly determine specifically what is expected of you.

- Interview the relevant key players—such as the Director of Human Resources or the executive who hired you and perhaps some employees who interact with your coaching clients—to learn more about the culture of the organization and recent changes or challenges.

- Identify the strengths your clients appreciate about themselves.

- Uncover the gaps between where they are and where they want to be.

- Clarify the goals of coaching.

- Clarify your coaching philosophy and ground rules for success.

CHALLENGING AND MOTIVATING CLIENTS

Clients ultimately will choose what they want to accomplish or what they want to change. Research has demonstrated that people will go through the motions as if they care about learning something or changing a behavior, but if they don't have a strong interest in the learning or the change, they will proceed to forget the learning or disregard it. Even if a person is coerced to change his or her behavior, once the coercion is removed, behavior will revert to its original state.[3] So the million-dollar question is, how do you help clients acquire or increase the motivation to change self-defeating behaviors?

Part of the answer is to help your clients increase their awareness of where they are now, the impact of their behaviors on themselves and others, and any incongruencies between their current situation and their values and dreams. In effect, you help clients recognize any dissonance so that they can become aware of the discomfort of being incongruent. With that awareness, clients then create the intention to decrease the gap between where they are and where they want to be. They can plan and learn how to do more of what will be helpful and less of what is interfering with their success. Further, as the coach, you help your clients take responsibility for their current situation and craft a positive intention to improve. Then you follow up with action planning and support.

To aid your clients in building internal alignment with their goals and motivation to achieve them, as a homework inquiry you might ask them to complete this sentence: "I am a person who . . . "

Challenging and Motivating Executive Clients
Paul Best, Ph.D., MPEC, and Eileen Sunzeri, M.S.

A subsidiary of a Fortune 500 company wanted to implement a major change initiative with the following objectives:

- increasing the effectiveness and quality of its internal processes

- increasing employee involvement and participation in decision making and problem solving

- increasing focus on meeting customers' quality and delivery requirements

- improving the profitability of the company

Our assignment was to work with the executive charged with implementing the overall change process and the other executives, managers, and supervisors on the behavior changes they would have to manifest to help the organization achieve a significant culture change. They could not just work harder, as they had in the past, but had to learn new and, in many cases, very uncomfortable behaviors that helped enlist the organization in the new behaviors and ways of working. The skills involved—all of which were focused on the change vision—included helping their teams to develop and communicate a compelling vision and strategy; delegation; participative problem solving; building a leading coalition; performance measurement; and recognition.

We worked one-on-one with executives, managers, and supervisors to help them gain appreciation for the impact of their behavior and develop strategies for increasing the effectiveness of their behavior given the organization's direction and the needs of their people. We also coached teams on how to work together to improve planning, communication, recognition, and problem solving.

...continued on next page

Here is a typical exchange with an executive on how he or she could personally affect desired changes in the organization:

Coach: What could you do to generate support for the vision within your organization?

Client: I suppose I could ask more people to participate on the teams and require them all to develop action plans.

Coach: Are there any ways that you can personally generate more support?

Client: I could attend the team meetings to ensure that everyone is involved, but I can't attend every meeting to make sure people stay involved.

Coach: What do you think would keep them involved in changing their behavior?

Client: I'm not sure. When we have made changes in the past, people eventually went back to the old ways.

Coach: How did you and the other executives change your behavior?

Client: What do you mean?

Coach: For example, were people recognized, rewarded, or promoted for supporting the changes?

Client: Are you saying that we need to pay people extra to do their jobs?

Coach: For people to change the way they do things there has to be something in it for them. You may have to change the way you measure their performance and the way you give them feedback about their performance. Can you think of any ways to do that besides increasing their pay?

Client: I guess we could find the ones who are performing and look for ways to thank them.

Coach: What could you do personally?

Client: I can make sure that the reviews of my staff include specific actions relating to the vision.

Coach: What else can you do to have an impact on the rest of your organization?

Client: I'm not sure . . .

Coach: How often do you thank people for doing a good job?

Client: We give employees' performance awards and a little celebration every five years of employment.

Coach: We know from research that the impact of recognition increases the closer it comes to the behavior you are trying to affect. Five-year celebrations are not only too far apart but may not be associated with specific performance that is helping you achieve your vision.

Client: The company doesn't provide any way to recognize people more often.

Coach: Are there ways you could do it yourself?

Client: I could hold recognition celebrations more often.

Coach: What about just thanking people who are making an impact on the desired changes?

Client: That feels a little artificial to me, and it would make me uncomfortable.

Coach: What about it makes you uncomfortable?

Client: Just saying thank you for the company feels hokey and possibly insincere.

Coach: Do you sincerely appreciate people who support your strategies and plans?

Client: Of course.

Coach: What if you just expressed that to them?

Client: You mean tell them that I personally appreciate what they are doing?

Coach: Assuming you do appreciate it, could you say it sincerely?

Client: If I just spoke to them individually and related specifically to what they had done.

Coach: Great! That will have a bigger impact than you think. Can you commit to trying it several times in the coming days?

Client: If I tie it to specific strategies we are currently focusing on, I could find some people whose actions are supportive and thank them.

Coach: How many would be reasonable for you to try to recognize in the next week?

Client: I will try to recognize three people over the next week.

Coach: When we meet next week, can we talk about how it worked out, what changes you would make, and whether it is something you could continue?

Client: OK.

The concept of thanking people for a job well done does not come naturally to a lot of executives. The kind of exchange depicted here often results in a trial period in which the executive discovers the impact of his or her informal recognition and then begins to have staff members act similarly. When executives change their behavior, the change can have a powerful effect on the organization, but they have to keep it up and not revert to their previous behavior patterns.

In this case, the coaching focus was on providing feedback for current behavior through observation and input from others and then helping the leaders develop their own plan to be successful in the new culture and to help their teams be successful. The results? The people in the company were very motivated to help the company change. Some of the leaders were able to make the changes and achieve significant success toward the company objectives. They were rewarded with new opportunities both inside and outside of the company.

MENTAL GUIDELINES FOR COACHES

Coaches need an internal perspective that will shape the questions they pose to clients to further the coaching agenda. The nature of the coach's mindset and the resulting questions and comments to the client will shape the coaching alliance. For example, the coach's internal perspective will aid in the generation of creative coaching inquiries that are tailored to a client's specific situation. Furthermore, the appropriate coaching mindset will translate into the coach being perceived by others as highly competent and sincerely engaged.

The following mental guidelines can help facilitate effective coaching and a positive coaching alliance.

Have a mindset of exploring how you can help your clients remove obstacles to their success. What barriers do they encounter? What are their ideas, and your ideas, about how the obstacles can be negotiated? How can their strengths and peak experiences be helpful?

Orient the conversation toward brainstorming, exploring the rationale behind the client's current thinking, and identifying appropriate goals and doable action steps. In general, steer away from exploring the psychological hooks that could lead to a path of exploring weakness and in turn bolster self-doubts. Instead, reinforce positive steps to build confidence, provide or foster extra support when difficulties warrant, and reframe past struggles as learning that now has value.

Reframe "problems" as "challenges." As clients describe their challenges, listen for and explore any patterned repetition. If you observe a repetition of behavior that often leads to unwanted consequences, this is a clue to explore the client's underlying thinking—or possibly, in the case of executive coaching, the organization's underlying thinking. When you help the client explore the thinking or rationale, new possibilities or reframes may occur to handle the challenge with improved outcomes.

As you listen to your clients' ideas, listen for the underlying rationale, concerns, and feeling. Notice any urge you have to give advice and consider whether inquiry would be more useful. (Inquiry as a technique is discussed in the next chapter.) Commit yourself to deep, active listening and develop a communication style that lets your clients know you understand their perspective. Listen for cognitive distortions or assumptions that may hinder your client's progress.

Communicate your commitment to assist clients with the coaching process. Trust in the idea that success will come when a coach speaks sincerely, honestly, and skillfully, and with high emotional intelligence, to an emotionally healthy client, even if at times the feedback you are giving is uncomfortable for you. Include compassion and emotional energy, when appropriate, in your communication style.

Think about how you can help clients open their eyes to reality while maintaining your rapport. Clients in coaching tend to have more ego strength than therapy clients, so you are empowered to speak more directly, helping them see not only possibilities but also how their actions may have been limiting their progress. Adopt a commitment to communicate consistent, open, and honest feedback against a background of extensive positive support when clients are ignoring or are blind to self-defeating patterns.

At select times, consider aiding your client in moving toward breakthrough processes rather than incremental improvement. Hargrove advocates using a three-step "breakthrough strategy" of (1) defining extraordinary results, (2) practicing "systematic abandonment" of things that aren't working, and (3) doing something different.[4] In executive coaching, for example, you can ask:

- "What extraordinary result needs to be achieved?"

- "What business approach needs to be abandoned because of its limiting effects on profits or production?"

- "Now that we have abandoned what is limiting, what are brainstorms to produce the extraordinary result?"

Also in executive coaching, help your client to improve the feedback that customers and employees are providing. Tremendous information on business improvement is missed because most organizations do not have a workable feedback process to decision makers. Here are some relevant coaching questions:

- "What powerful feedback pathways do you have in place from your customers to decision makers?"

- "In what ways is feedback encouraged between front-line employees and decision makers?"

- "What rewards are given to employees or customers for feedback and suggestions?"

- "What do you want to see happen related to improving feedback from customers and employees?"

SUMMARY

A powerful coaching alliance is rooted in a relationship of mutual trust and respect. The initial manner in which you contract with the client serves as a springboard into the deeper elements of developing a mutually successful working relationship. The questionnaires, agreements, and assessments that you use to gather useful information about your client also provide you with discussion material to help shape the early coaching sessions. Incorporating the assessment results and your own observations, you can adapt your communication and questioning style to best fit the natural preferences of your client.

Understanding the client's world view and patterns of thinking is critical to the development of a successful coaching alliance. Your ability to detect clients' blindspots and introduce new perspectives and language into their thinking will enable them to continue progressing after the coaching relationship is concluded.

Coaching requires you to build trust quickly, especially when your contact with clients is over the telephone. Trust is built primarily by your actions (for example, meticulousness in following through with basic professional details) and your style of communication (for example, a style that communicates warmth, empathy, and a basic trust in your clients' ability to do what they say they can do).

Behavioral change requires genuine internal commitment. In order to help clients stay motivated with their coaching agenda, help them increase their awareness of where they are versus where they want to be and of the effects of their actions on others. Focus on clients' taking responsibility for their own situations.

Your mindset as a coach will guide your questions and feedback to clients. Maintain a mindset of building on your clients' strengths and successes while you help them decrease negative outcomes from any blindspots. Stay in touch with the positive, forward-looking nature of coaching with fundamentally healthy clients, as opposed to wearing your therapist hat. Your task is to help clients advance to a new level of skill or personal development. When you combine this coaching mindset with the tools provided in the next chapter, you have the formula to help your clients move forward quickly.

Coaching Techniques

Outstanding coaches, like outstanding therapists, undergo a lifetime of learning and personal growth. Coaches are effective because of who they are, combined with appropriate technique. This chapter describes numerous techniques and the language that coaches utilize. Some of the techniques will be relatively easy to add to your repertoire of skills, based on the material provided here. Other techniques will require you to take specific training courses to enable you to learn the skills, practice the techniques, and receive feedback on their application from experienced graduate-level coaches.

A COACHING SCHEMATIC

To help you get "your hands on" the coaching process and guide your coaching, you can internalize an eight-point coaching schematic.[1] As a coach, keep in mind that you are:

1. Helping your clients clarify their passions and goals
2. Enlisting their passions into the coaching
3. Helping your clients organize their thoughts
4. Clarifying expectations and outcomes
5. Providing rapid, straightforward feedback
6. Helping your clients build their capabilities
7. Recognizing openings for coaching
8. Building accountability and reinforcement

With this schematic in mind, here are some questions you can ask yourself to help guide your conversations with your clients.

"What can I ask or say to . . ."

- "help my clients unleash their aspirations?"

- "increase their personal and business success?"

- "clarify ways in which they are thinking or acting that might be producing unintended consequences?"

- "facilitate important learning for their situation?"

- (in some executive coaching situations)"aid in enhanced team functioning?"

ASSESSMENT

Assessment tools can add considerable value to coaching performed by mental health professionals. Leaders in the executive development field, such as the international nonprofit organization Center for Creative Leadership, make the assessment process an integral part of the early coaching experience. Using assessments in coaching is often referred to as "instrumented coaching." However, assessments must always be used to complement other interactions with clients and should never be used as the sole basis for developing a coaching agenda. You will read more about assessments and coaching in Chapter 7.

PERMISSION AND COMMITMENT

Both the client and the coach need to be committed to the coaching relationship and proposed coaching outcomes for the relationship to be most effective. Some clients may come to coaching because they have been requested by their supervisor or manager to receive coaching, or because they think that it is the right thing to do. However, if there isn't an internal commitment, also called an "enrollment" in the coaching process, the client is likely to find the experience rather flat and devoid of passion, which could lead to premature termination of coaching or a poor outcome.

James Flaherty observes that enrollment in effective coaching involves "an active dialogue that takes into account the particulars of the circumstances, the vagaries of the future, and the limitations and strengths of both the client and coach. Openness, honesty, and completeness are vital in enrollment."[2] To this we can add Robert Hargrove's observation that when clients and coaches ask themselves, "Who am I?" and "What can I do here that I passionately care about?" they build internal commitment to their work.[3]

According to Hargrove, three coaching steps reinforce internal commitment:

- engaging in a conversation about personal, and sometimes, organizational, vision

- having clients create goals they are passionate about

- having clients design their own plans, combined with self-directed learning[4]

Commitment is closely related to the concept of permission. Successful coaching with an emotionally engaged client starts as soon as the client gives permission to be coached. Permission means "to make possible or to give opportunity." Without the client giving permission, there will not be a commitment to the coaching.

Accordingly, early on in the coaching relationship, after a discussion about what coaching is, the coach may ask the client, "Now that we have talked a little bit about coaching, are you willing to have me coach you?" Also, there will be times when sensitive subjects may be brought up. At such times the coach can preface comments with, "May

I tell you what I think?" or "How about we brainstorm together other possible courses of action?"[5]

In addition to granting permission to the coach, clients also have to give *themselves* permission to open up about their dreams and challenges, and to invest time and money in themselves. Later in the process of coaching, clients may need to give themselves permission to take specific actions, for example, to make more money or to take more time off from work.

The concept of permission applies to coaches as well. Coaches need to give themselves permission to be open, honest, and forthcoming with their clients. At times coaches may need to give themselves permission to give feedback that is not easy for them to deliver. It is helpful early in the coaching relationship to talk about the process of permission, when and where it comes up and how it will be handled. At that point it is wise to discuss that there might be times for both coach and client to give feedback they may not be easy to deliver. Furthermore, it would be helpful to include in your dialogue with your client the following request: "I've found it is a useful practice to give each other permission to go ahead and give each other complete and honest feedback whenever it is called for."

HOMEWORK INQUIRIES

Inquiry is the process of asking powerful questions that require reflection. Inquiries are formed based on the client's particular situation. Inquiries always involve introspection, and they may also involve intuition, sensing, and creativity. Homework inquiries are used as an assignment, in between coaching sessions, to deepen the process of personal discovery and learning. Midway through or near the end of a coaching session, the coach, or the client, may formulate an inquiry for the client to ponder as a homework assignment. Here are several inquiries as examples:

- "How have you overcome obstacles like this in the past?"

- "If a wizard appeared and granted one wish for the next chapter of your life, what would it be?"

- "What is your dream of an ideal life?"

- "How can you change how you spend time in a way that supports your values?"

- "If you could have any three amazing advisors, living or deceased, to guide the next chapter of your life, who would they be?"

- "What limiting self-talk are you aware of?"

- "What are three of your most important strengths?"

- "In what ways are your strengths important? What are some examples of how they are important to you?"

- "If you were to receive a gift of money to fund the next phase of your life, how much would that be?"

- "If you were at your highest level of living right now, how would you be doing things differently?"

- "Imagine yourself with a heart full of courage. What would you do?"

- "Tune into an experience you had in the past when you overcame a challenge or a fear and excelled. Bring that feeling of accomplishment forward with you now and ask yourself, What major goal do you want to move forward with?"

- "If you could eliminate all fear, what would you do now?"

Homework inquiries are useful to deepen the coaching process and to take the coaching from within the formal appointment time into the client's day-to-day life. Between coaching sessions many clients will write journal entries on the inquiry and send the coach an e-mail of their thinking. To help a client to reflect on the inquiry, you may ask how the client will remember to work on it. Common approaches are to schedule a walk or a visit to the beach, or to put up notes to remind oneself to reflect on the inquiry.

The response to the inquiry can then be followed the next week with questions designed to formulate action steps. For example, "How have you overcome obstacles like this in the past?" can be followed by "Building on that past success, what is your best step to take this week?" Or "What are your three most important strengths?" can be followed by "What is one new way this week that you can use that strength to help you in business?"

APPRECIATIVE INQUIRY

Wouldn't it be exciting, and a relief, if instead of looking for dysfunction, as some do in a medical model of psychotherapy, we spent considerable time looking for our clients' highest, most exciting, and invigorating peak experiences and helped them learn how to build on them? As you have seen, that is what much of coaching is all about, and it is the basis of the technique called "appreciative inquiry."

Appreciative inquiry is a process of asking "What is working well?" After clients have been helped to focus on a positive core of life experiences, they are then guided through a creative conversation to explore "what might be" and then "what will be."

The appreciative inquiry approach was originally developed by David Cooperrider and his associates at the Weatherhead School of Management, Case Western Reserve University.[6] In recent years the principles and practices of appreciative inquiry have been used to dramatically improve results at corporations such as GTE, Ameritech, McDonald's, and John Deere. Originally used as a progressive organizational development tool, appreciative inquiry is now being used in individual coaching.

Sue Hammond writes, in the *Thin Book of Appreciative Inquiry*, that traditionally in organizational or personal development work the focus is on defining the problem, fixing what is broken, and learning from mistakes.[7] She presents appreciative inquiry as a shift from a problem focus to a search for solutions that already exist and to learning from what works. Instead of asking, "What problems are you having?" we can ask, "What is working around here?"

The appreciative inquiry process is a powerful model to help the client, or the organization, move forward. The model has five stages, often known as the five D's:

1. *Define* the need for development and the scope of the inquiry, agreeing to focus on the positive.

2. *Discover* information by an appreciative interview process.

3. *Dream* images for the future.

4. *Design* achievable steps to make the vision a reality.

5. *Deliver* by establishing the who, what, when, and how of the changes that will be implemented.[8]

Using appreciative inquiry early in the coaching process can help get you started with clients on a path of positive change as you forge a relationship that builds on the client's strengths and peak experiences. For example, you might ask a client, "What learning have you appreciated from dealing with some of the biggest problems or challenges you have faced?" A question like this can uncover the significant growth and meaning that an individual might have experienced through successfully coping with tragedy such as the loss of a loved one. Here are other examples of using appreciative inquiry that can be appropriate in the initial stages of coaching:

- "Tell me a story about a time in your life when you felt particularly joyful, creative, successful—a real high point. Make yourself the hero or heroine of the story. Describe the event in detail. What made it an exciting experience? Who was involved? Describe how you felt … Describe what you did as a result of the experience."

- "Without being humble, tell me what it is that you value most about yourself."

Utilizing this process model, coaches can develop other appreciative inquiries with their clients. A series of provocative propositions that describe a preferred vision of the future is one result of the inquiry process. This preferred vision is grounded in the highest moments of the participants' lives, so that clients have a sense that they can achieve similar successes again. Appreciative inquiry participants often experience dynamic memories of success that fuel enthusiastic energy for their current work or life challenges.

Coaching in the Appreciative Zone
Robert J. Voyle, Psy.D., MPEC

I came to coaching via the path of being an Episcopal priest and a clinical psychologist. Metaphorically you could say it was the path of sin and sickness. Most interventions in both fields were focused on discovering what was wrong and then applying some corrective strategy. Many sessions, for example, would occur with the unspoken agreement that something was wrong. Such sessions might even begin with the words "What's wrong?" Sometimes people were helped and sometimes things just got worse.

The fact that things sometimes got worse caused me to

…continued on next page

---

continue searching to find ways of interacting with church members or clients that affirmed their dignity as human beings and enabled them to be liberated rather than continually oppressed. That search has taken me to the path of contemplative spirituality and writers like Thomas Merton, and positive psychology as demonstrated by people like Milton Erickson and the appreciative inquiry of people like David Cooperrider and his associates. Metaphorically I would call my synthesis of these approaches when working with clients or groups "Coaching in the Appreciative Zone."

I think of coaching as enabling clients to access the resources they need to respond creatively to their current or future life demands. The vast majority of these resources are located within the client. Even external resources are dependent on a client's internal resource of being able to effectively ask for assistance.

Most clinicians have had the experience of an entire treatment session coming unhinged because at one critical moment they said something or did something that took the client down a path of no apparent positive return. Conversely, most clinicians have also had the experience of saying something at a critical junction that resulted in a release within the client of a liberating creativity that was beyond either of their wildest imaginations. When I reflect on my own experiences of these critical moments, I can see that what was most important in facilitating a creative experience was that I managed to stay in the appreciative zone rather than become frightened and retreating to a problem focused approach. In the appreciative zone both client and coach can compassionately behold the client and value his or her skills, abilities, and experiences that result in the manifestation of the unique resources that can be brought to bear on the client's challenges.

Staying in the appreciative zone is not always easy. The big enemy is always fear. For example, fear may arise that the session is not working well or that the client's situation is overwhelming. The other enemy is our past training and focus on sin or sickness and living in a culture that is saturated with notions of blame

…continued on next page

and judgment. Fortunately the positive fruits of the appreciative zone are inspiring and serve as an enlightening teacher, as the following example shows.

I was coaching a client to balance a myriad of family, work, and school demands. She had identified several personal experiences that could serve as resources to be applied to her challenge. As part of the coaching, she was going through an imaginative process whereby she could imagine facing her many challenges and envision herself maintaining both the attitudes and emotions that she desired as she responded to the demands. In the midst of the exercise it became apparent from the nuances of her reactions that she was becoming quite conflicted and distressed and not at all experiencing the emotions that she desired.

My natural instinct, on sensing the sudden distress, was to ask, "What's wrong?" Fortunately the seed of appreciation had taken root within me and I was able to stifle the instinctual response and ask "What other resource or resources do you need to manage the demands?" She quickly was able to identify a novel way she had dealt with a parallel situation and how she could use it in dealing with her current demands, despite the fact that it was contrary to the typical advice of experts in her field. Her internal conflict had resulted from trying to manage her demands in a manner that was contrary to her own basic nature and her own proven strategies. As she reclaimed this resource, she was able to rehearse several scenarios of increasing complexity while maintaining her sense of balance, confidence, and joy.

Such experiences in themselves may appear minor, but they water the small seeds of the positive approach and enable it to grow. They inspire confidence in the enormous potential within each client to creatively meet the demands of his or her life. We do not need to waste time figuring out what is wrong and who is to blame. Rather, we can entrust our clients to their own life-giving resources and mutually enjoy the creative possibilities of the appreciative zone.

VALUES CLARIFICATION

What ensures that the coaching process is powerful and deeply satisfying to the client? By ensuring that the coaching agenda is congruent with the client's most important values, a fundamental depth to the coaching is created. Otherwise, the coaching would ultimately have a superficial feel. A coaching agenda rooted in the client's leading values generates commitment and purpose. In turn, purpose and commitment translate into motivation.

According to Louis Raths and colleagues, the process of valuing is composed of three processes and six subprocesses:

Process One: Prizing one's beliefs and behavior

1. Prizing and cherishing
2. Publicly affirming, when it is appropriate

Process Two: Choosing one's beliefs and behaviors

1. Choosing from alternatives
2. Choosing after consideration of consequences
3. Choosing freely

Process Three: Acting on one's beliefs

1. Acting with a pattern, consistency, and repetition.[9]

John Murphy and Frederic Hudson's research of hundreds of successful adults found that the prominence of particular values changes over an individual's lifetime.[10] They also found that most successful individuals are actively engaged with no more than three of these value groupings in one phase of their life. Furthermore, the particular values that are most prominent in one's life often shift over time; for example, a twenty-five year old's value focus often differs from a sixty year old's.[11]

Here are the six core values Hudson describes:

1. Personal power—knowing yourself

2. Achievement—reaching your goals

3. Intimacy—loving and being loved

4. Play and creativity—expressing yourself

5. Search for meaning—integrating yourself

6. Compassion and legacy—repairing the world[12]

I usually have my client complete a values-clarification process for homework within the first few sessions. (A sample values-clarification exercise is in the Appendix.) Typically, I provide my clients with a list of value terms and ask them to find a quiet time to consider the value words on the list and add any other of their own. Next, I ask them to list their ten or twelve most important values and group the value words that seem to fit together congruently on one line. For example, the client might create a list like this one:

> *Family/Friendship*
> *Zest/Integrity/Authenticity*
> *Productivity/Excellence/Collaboration/Success*

Next, I ask the client to narrow the value list down to the top three most important values in this chapter of his or her life. The client might then come up with this list:

> *Family*
> *Integrity*
> *Excellence*

My clients usually find this a powerful and useful experience. With their values clarified (this process can be revisited periodically—perhaps every few months) clients can measure their coaching agenda for congruency with their most important values. You may ask your client, "How does this goal fit in with your most important values?" or "As a way of analyzing the pros and cons of your possible decision, tell me about how this action you are contemplating complements your values."

LIFE BALANCE TECHNIQUES

You will frequently hear people describe themselves as "life balance coaches." I don't advocate labeling yourself in this way because life balance coaches are common. If you are going to label yourself, pick a unique niche that no one else has.

That said, a considerable amount of many coaching relationships include helping clients restore balance to their lives and take good care of themselves, in line with their highest values. In this connection my clients have found two techniques especially helpful: reducing energy drains and taking "ultradian" breaks.

In her best-selling book *Take Time for Your Life*, Cheryl Richardson writes about the value of reducing "energy drains"—ways in which one's life force seems to be drained away.[13] An energy drain can be something as simple as having piles of papers stacked up in your office or as profound as the realization that you feel stuck in a job that is antithetical to your values. In coaching, you can help your clients assess their lives for the many ways their energy may be drained and then help them develop a coaching plan to create a more ideal situation. Thomas Leonard describes an assessment called the CleanSweep™ Program, in which clients assess one hundred areas of their lives with items such as "My personal files, papers, and receipts are neatly filed away," "I currently live well within my means," and "I quickly correct misunderstandings when they occur."[14]

Identifying several energy-draining areas in a client's life can help create an early coaching agenda. After some of those bothersome problems are resolved, clients have more energy to pursue their loftier goals.

Ernest Rossi has elaborated extensively on how humans have natural rest/activity cycles that continue twenty-four hours a day.[15] Rossi, who worked closely with Milton Erickson, M.D., noted that much of the sensational learning and behavioral change that Erickson was able to help clients generate came by capitalizing on the healing and learning potential that can result from following naturally occurring variations in consciousness.[16] We are all aware of the important health effects of sleep and how we progress through its various stages. Rossi points out that we also have "ultradian rhythms," or physiological cycles that occur several times every twenty-four hours. In particular, we have naturally occurring "dip times" during the day, when we find ourselves yawning and our concentration wanes. When we tune into these times and let ourselves close our eyes and rest for fifteen minutes, we feel rejuvenated, clear-headed, and healthier.

To help people maintain peak performance I often educate clients to notice their naturally occurring alert and drowsy times of the day. Then I coach them to let themselves take a ten-to-twenty-minute break, at the stage of drowsiness, to allow themselves to naturally "recharge their batteries." I have found that clients who implement "ultradian breaks" perform better and report improved mood and energy levels. Most clients who practice this approach find they have increased energy, concentration, and performance without the side effects associated with drinking beverages with caffeine or snacking on sugar-laden treats.

Coaching for Peak Performance

Sandra Foster, Ph.D., MPEC

Brenda Wong Aoki is a spoken-word artist who combines Noh and Kabuki theater traditions, storytelling, modern dance, and personal experience in her one-woman performance pieces. (Ms. Aoki gave her permission for her name to be used in this vignette.) Born into working class circumstances in Los Angeles, Brenda learned of her illustrious samurai heritage while researching her Japanese great uncle's scandalous 1910 marriage to the daughter of the San Francisco Episcopal archbishop. Her discovery of this first Asian American marriage in California inspired Uncle Gunjiro's Girlfriend, which premiered in 1998. (Ms. Aoki is a recipient of National Endowment for the Arts grants and has enjoyed considerable critical acclaim for her work, including the 1997 Golden Ring Award for Asian American artists.)

This client sought performance coaching in 1997 during the expansion of her repertoire into, as she described it, a wider "mainstream Caucasian" audience. When she called me, she was rehearsing a new performance piece entitled Mermaid that was to be accompanied by the Berkeley (California) Symphony Orchestra. Brenda's husband, Mark Izu, composed the music and would be playing the sho, a Japanese multireed wind instrument. Brenda's friend Kent Nagano, Musical Director for the Symphony, would be conducting.

Brenda expressed the following concerns in our initial meetings (ten and eleven weeks prior to the premiere):

1. The tremendous time pressure in the weeks preceding opening night for Mark to finish the musical score and for Brenda to complete the final version of her script.

2. Her worry about sustaining her success (and tour schedule) as she was reaching a new level of recognition by mainstream audiences.

...continued on next page

3. Her fear that achieving this level of fame would leave her feeling "guilty," as if she were leaving behind her "people in the barrio," those whom she had known from her neighborhood and whose stories she portrayed in her earlier dramatic pieces.

4. Her uncertainty about the source from which she would draw her inspiration and energy for Mermaid, the dark and dramatic Japanese story she had authored.

5. Her negative ruminations about the reaction of a primarily Caucasian audience and the critics to the portrayal of such a story and to the sound of Japanese instruments being played with the full orchestra.

From this list of concerns, Brenda defined her goals for the coaching: "to manage myself well emotionally through rehearsals; to be totally into the performance on opening night; to handle distractions well during rehearsals; and to move from uncertainty, even guilt, about my success to really pursuing opportunities for my work (greater distribution of my CD's, writing the book on Gunjiro, and securing a screenplay of Queen's Garden or Random Acts of Kindness [earlier productions]."

I used a combination of strategies in my coaching with Brenda:

- Socratic questioning drawn from my training in cognitive therapy, particularly "what" and "how" open-ended questions. Examples were "How will it be different in a symphony environment to coordinate your tech crew?" and "What can help you sustain your physical conditioning for this role?"

- Strategic visioning to help articulate Brenda's desired future.

- EMDR-integrated coaching (a protocol I developed in 1991 in collaboration with colleague Jennifer Lendl, Ph.D.).[17]

...continued on next page

- Refining, in a deliberate fashion in my office, Brenda's customary imagery and movement work to assist her in creating the desired performance state.

- Coaching Brenda in peak performance skills, especially distraction management aimed at enhancing her focusing capacity.

Eleven hours of in-office coaching was all that was possible given Brenda's demanding schedule of editing, rehearsing, physical conditioning, teaching, costume fitting, grant writing for other projects, organizing the technical aspects of the performance, and parenting her young son. Initially, I reviewed her current use of time and coached her in tactics for coping with the overload while guarding her contemplative hours. Viewing earlier works on video and attending the first practice run-through of Mermaid helped me be more on target, having witnessed Brenda's craft for myself.

Out of the EMDR-integrated coaching in particular emerged Brenda's awareness that she did not have to isolate herself from her family as her fame grew among wider audiences. She realized that her fear of success arose from a lingering sense of herself as the "kid from the Long Beach ghetto" who cared for five sisters and worried with her parents when money was scarce. She began to perceive herself not as a lonely star separated from her "people" but as a successful intercultural voice still connected to them all and able to share her newfound abundance with her family.

Brenda sought a means for viewing her Berkeley symphony audience as similar to her. Our questioning led her to the view that "we are alike because we all share a heart and blood." Applying the metaphor of blood and pulsating energy, Brenda wove together a rich fabric of images of a volcano with its pulsing lava flow. Her "key words" for her performance became "I'm performing in the Belly of Mother Earth, within all Her energy, fire and love."

...continued on next page

> *While Brenda practiced her tactics for remaining focused on stage and managing her fear, she visualized herself at the foot of the volcano and also as an iconic image nearby, representing "all the women who have come before." These images were both empowering and grounding for her.*
>
> *Opening night finally arrived. The audience around me seemed mesmerized by Brenda's dramatic vocalizing and powerful, sensual movements, and rose to their feet in a lengthy ovation. The following day, critics wrote glowingly about the premiere. One concluded there would be a "definite future on classical music stages for such artful blends of Western theatricality with Japanese Noh and Kyogen drama." (Cheryl North, correspondent for the Oakland Tribune).*

EFFECTIVE FEEDBACK

In Chapter 1, I referred to a study of seventy-five executives who identified honest, reliable feedback as one of the most important elements of effective coaching.[18] Feedback is information that you provide in your coaching conversation that clients use to help them evaluate if they are on track and to help them adjust or correct their thinking if they are headed down the wrong road. To be useful, feedback needs to be honest and reliable, that is, given consistently. It also needs to be specifically tied to some event or idea with sufficient attention to detail to make it specific and not generic.

Coaches who can deliver concise messages on what they observe in their clients' behavior offer tremendous value for their clients' learning. In addition, in executive coaching, teaching your clients how to give effective feedback to others may be critical for their success. But how do you offer feedback that is effective, clear, and phrased in such a way that it can be heard well?

Principles of Sound Feedback

Coaches can deliver powerful, effective messages by making them especially clear, specific, and useful by following sound feedback principles. Consider these messages that are not particularly helpful to clients:

- "You're doing great."

- "You're being too demanding."

- "You always say ..."

What is wrong with "You're doing great"? Being supportive is helpful, but this feedback is too vague. Vague supportive feedback may make the client feel good, but it doesn't contribute to any particular learning because the client may not be clear about what actions or behavior lead to being "great." Instead, be specific: "You are doing great to have already asked for three volunteers to help you on the new project that you started yesterday."

What is the problem with giving the feedback, "You're being too demanding"? This remark sounds judgmental of the individual rather than useful, specific feedback on a particular behavior in a particular situation. As you would expect, this type of feedback is likely to engender defensiveness. The result is that extra time and energy are consumed in dealing with the person's feeling that he or she is being judged unfairly. Instead, the coach could say, "When I sat in on your meeting yesterday, I noticed you raising your voice, leaning over the table, and jabbing your finger at Jim, while saying, 'I need this right away, I don't care what else you are doing!' What effect do you think that incident had on Jim?"

Finally, feedback of the form "You always . . ." is also likely to prompt a defensive reaction as the person immediately begins thinking of exceptions rather than focusing on the message the coach is trying to communicate.

Apart from poorly phrased feedback, another common problem that people have when they give feedback is they speak for too long. The individual receiving the feedback needs time to absorb the feedback, reflect on it, and decide whether or not he or she agrees. When you deliver concise, specific messages, the client is free to evaluate what you have said and a dialogue can then occur.

These ideas lead to some general tips for increasing the relevance and effectiveness of your feedback to clients:

- Specifically describe the situation and the action. Use actual quotes if possible.

- Comment on the idea or the behavior, not the person.

- Give feedback in the moment, if appropriate.

- Be as specific as possible.

- Describe the result of the behavior on you.

- Focus on a single message so you don't dilute your message.

- Provide feedback in a concise manner to allow for dialogue.

- Realize that your feedback may have an emotional impact.

These guidelines are capsulized in the STAR Technique, described next.

The STAR Technique

The STAR Technique consists of three steps: Specific Target, Action, and Results.

The first step, "Specific Target," means that you identify the specific situation that you are giving feedback about. Describe the time and place. For example, "You know, Bob, I was thinking about how at the beginning of our phone call today, you described the discussion you had with your plant manager . . ."

The second step is to describe the specific "Action" or behavior that you are giving feedback about. For example, "You said you noticed a warm feeling inside yourself and that you were smiling when you praised your plant manager for rewarding his staff with gift certificates . . . "

The third step is to discuss the "Result" that the specific target situation and action have on you. You describe the effect the situation had on you because that is more powerful than talking about what effect you suppose it may have had on others. Continuing the above example, "I felt excited inside, and I was smiling to myself, as I heard about how you were following through on your plan of getting out of your office every day and visiting your employees."

By giving feedback in this manner, you provide clients with specific examples so they will have the benefit of knowing exactly what progress you see them making or what areas they need to work on. This style of providing feedback also serves as a model of how your clients can provide effective feedback to their peers, bosses, and subordinates.

HOLDING THE FOCUS OF THE CLIENT'S AGENDA

Have you had the experience of having great ideas about things you wanted to accomplish in your career or personal life and then finding that you didn't accomplish them because other pressing situations arose? Perhaps you didn't stay focused because other attractive options arose and you couldn't get everything done. A coach helps clients clarify that their goals are important goals, aligned with their vision and purpose, and then helps them stay on track with their self-designed agenda. For some individuals—strategic or idealistic entrepreneurs, for example—endless exciting business opportunities may occur to them. The danger is that by adding too many projects to their plate they dilute their ability to maintain focus, take action, and progress on their strategic plan. As a coach, you presume your clients have the answers within them, and you facilitate a dialogue that helps them remain focused on their current plan, or with conscious awareness evaluate whether they should make a change to their plan.

This is where you step in with realistic feedback and questioning to help clients evaluate for themselves: "What is the best use of your time? In what ways does this idea fit with your strategic life plan? When you look at your calendar and consider scheduling your actions, how does this idea enhance or hinder your movement toward your goals?"

Clients' coaching agendas are usually rooted in their values of what they want most from their lives. Your clients' intentions are likely to be admirable, but life will put them to the test. It is easier for clients to maintain focus on their own agendas when you consciously hold their agendas in your mind and engage in coaching conversations that support them in staying true to course.

For example, a client may say that he wants to spend more time with his children but that his job requires him to travel more. The additional income and prestige of career success are alluring and powerful. However, as a coach you help your client align his values, remember his self-designed coaching agenda, and discover and explore heretofore undeveloped options. Thus you may ask: "Thomas, we both remember that one of your overarching values in this phase of your life is increasing quality time with your children. How will the decision to accept this new project affect that value?"

Of course, there may be powerful reasons the client feels obliged to accept increased travel. Perhaps one of his commitments is to double his contribution to the family college fund. In these kinds of circumstances you may need to be tenacious: "Since you feel it is important to take this on, Thomas, in what creative ways can you continue to move forward with increasing family time?" Perhaps you will go on to explore with the client letting go of another activity, delegating other responsibilities, or taking the family along on some of the trips.

Often clients have to choose an option that does interfere with the carefully designed coaching plan. The complexity of life and the rapid nature of change necessitate the need for renewed effort to focus on a designed agenda while also requiring adaptability, further increasing the value of professional coaches.

BOTTOM-LINING

One of the challenges therapists face when transitioning to coaching is their tendency to want to follow up on different hooks that the client's story suggests and to let a client go on too long with his or her story, resulting in less time for inquiry and creating the future.

Why do some clients tend to tell stories that can take over the whole session? Sometimes the tendency to tell long stories is the client's style of conversing. Sometimes clients tell their stories at length because they are avoiding a difficult issue. And some clients have personalities that push them to make sure the coach understands the "complete picture."

What do you do when clients' stories tend to take up most of the coaching session? "Bottom-lining" is the skill of helping clients get to the point (taking into account the client's and coach's communication style and preferences). To prepare the client to be able to get to the bottom line and thus get more learning and movement from the coaching sessions, bring up the concept of succinct communication in the first or second session.[19] You can say, for example, "Because our coaching sessions will usually be a half-hour, it is often helpful to be able to communicate any stories that are important to tell me rather succinctly so we have time to discuss how to take the learning from the story and apply it to moving closer to your goals. Sometimes I might ask you, 'What is the bottom line here?' or 'What is the essence of your challenge here?'"

The coach can also benefit from practicing succinct conversation. By getting to the bottom line in your own communication, you will model a purposeful communication style for your client and at the same time ensure that you don't dominate the coaching session. Of course, cultural issues may affect the desired conversation style, and it is important to not impose a style on a client that would break effective rapport.

LADDER OF INFERENCE

A useful tool in helping clients examine their thinking processes is the "ladder of inference" method, originally developed by Chris Argyris.[20] In executive coaching, the ladder of inference is probably the most commonly used, and most effective, technique to help executives evaluate and improve their cognition and communication in team settings. The ladder of inference is applicable in personal coaching as well.

The concept of the ladder of inference can help your clients identify the steps in their reasoning that may lead to unintended consequences. The ladder of inference focuses on how people come to take the actions they take. Here is how it works:

1. People first observe "data."
2. They then select data from what they have observed.
3. They add meaning to the data from a personal and cultural perspective.
4. They make assumptions based on the meaning that they have added.
5. They draw conclusions based on their assumptions.
6. They adopt beliefs based on their conclusions.
7. Finally, they take actions based on their conclusions.

Executive coaches Reldan Nadler and John Luckner have adapted Argyris's ladder of inference, simplifying the steps in a manner that many coaches have found to be easier to use with their clients. They call their version the "Assumption Ladder."[21] See Figures 1 and 2.

Thus, when people adamantly believe that their beliefs are the truth, that the truth is obvious—that their beliefs are based on real data and that the data selected are the real data—they may be headed for a conclusion that is unfounded and can create a myriad of unintended and avoidable consequences.

Coaches help clients manage the ladder of inference process by advocating these three guiding principles: (1) becoming more aware of one's own reasoning processes, (2) sharing one's reasoning with others, and (3) inquiring into other people's reasoning (for example, their colleagues, in organizational and team settings). People will have fewer misunderstandings, more collegial relationships in work environments, and fewer arguments in personal relationships when they have deeper understanding of the other person's thought process, therefore making fewer faulty assumptions about the other person's thinking. The coaching vignette "Ladder of Inference in Executive Coaching" illustrates how the ladder concept can help clients think differently and consequently act more effectively.

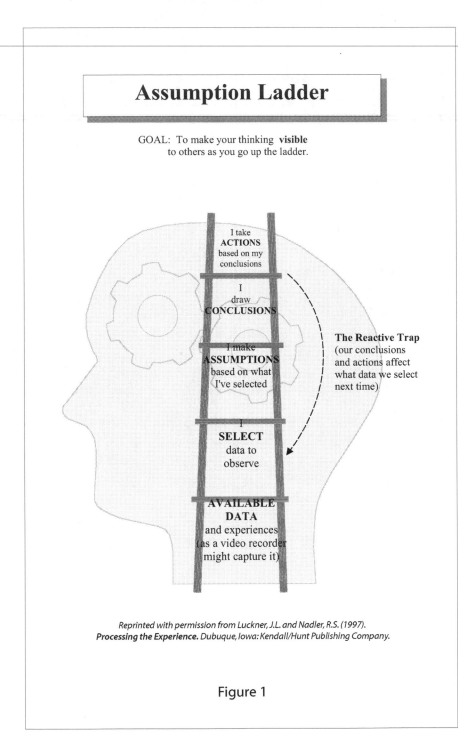

Assumption Ladder

GOAL: To make your thinking **visible**
to others as you go up the ladder.

I take
ACTIONS
based on my
conclusions

I
draw
CONCLUSIONS

I make
ASSUMPTIONS
based on what
I've selected

The Reactive Trap
(our conclusions
and actions affect
what data we select
next time)

I
SELECT
data to
observe

**AVAILABLE
DATA**
and experiences
(as a video recorder
might capture it)

Reprinted with permission from Luckner, J.L. and Nadler, R.S. (1997).
Processing the Experience. *Dubuque, Iowa: Kendall/Hunt Publishing Company.*

Figure 1

Assumption Ladder
Applications

Below are some examples of sentences and sentence stubs
that will help you walk up or down the ladder.

As a Listener:

I hear your actions.
What are they based on?
How did you arrive at these plans?

Tell me what conclusion you
are drawing....
Could it be possible that....

Tell me what you're assumptions
are....
I'm curious, tell me more....
Is that the only way to look at it?

What piece are you looking at?
I see you're focusing on....
What is standing out to you from
the data?

Give me all the facts...
What are all the findings?

As a Speaker:

Therefore, this is my plan....
These are steps I am taking....

It's obvious to me...
Therefore, I feel.... // As a result....
To summarize // Here we go again....

So, I'm assuming....
Here's what I attribute....
The next step for me is....

I am focusing on this piece....
Here's what I see happening....
Here's what I'm selecting.
This stands out to me....

Here are all the facts...
Here are all the findings...

ACTIONS

CONCLUSIONS

ASSUMPTIONS

SELECTED DATA

AVAILABLE

Pay attention to intentions // Make your thinking visible

Reprinted with permission from Luckner, J.L. and Nadler, R.S. (1997).
***Processing the Experience.** Dubuque, Iowa: Kendall/Hunt Publishing Company.*

Figure 2

Ladder of Inference in Executive Coaching

Jeffrey E. Auerbach, Ph.D., MPEC

I consulted with an organization that had just brought in a new division manager. He conducted his first team meeting, and I had a coaching session with one his staff afterwards.

My client related her observation of how the new manager, Russell, led their first meeting: "He spoke quickly and didn't smile." The client related how when she thought about the meeting she realized Russell seemed to be glaring at her, meaning he didn't like her, didn't think she was very smart, and didn't think she had anything to offer. She told me how she decided, "I'd better lay low. He doesn't like me and I don't want to call any attention to myself. I'm going to avoid going by his office unless he calls me."

My client had gone to the top of the ladder of inference after just one encounter with her new boss, based on one observable fact: "He spoke quickly and didn't smile." She selectively focused on this single piece of data, engaged in increasing abstraction, made assumptions on Russell's cognitions, drew conclusions, adopted beliefs, and planned actions. Unfortunately, the rapid mental process she traveled through led her to misguided conclusions and a terrible plan of action. Her rash plan would inadvertently lead to just what she feared—that Russell would conclude she wasn't offering anything to the group.

Once I explained the concept of the ladder of inference to my client, I was able to ask the following questions:

- "Of what you told me about the meeting, which parts are clearly observable factual data that I would be able to see or hear from videotape?"

- "Would you explain your reasoning to me of how you came to your conclusion about Russell?"

…continued on next page

- "What parts from what you described are clearly observable facts and what might be assumptions that you have made?"

My client was able to see that she was "jumping the gun" and that she was jeopardizing her job by planning on withdrawing rather than seeing the situation as an opportunity to create a positive relationship from a relatively clean slate.

OPENINGS

An opening is a time when coaching will be especially well received. Often, clients are especially "open" when they want something and they are not confident in how to achieve their desire, when they have a trusting relationship with their coach, and when there is rapport in the moment. In addition, openings occur when clients are in transition and want assistance navigating new territory, when they sense a new opportunity and want to make the most of it, and sometimes when they "hit the wall" or stumble. Sometimes a client will ask for coaching on a particular area; other times the coach will observe a potential for coaching. The idea is to time the suggestion of coaching to coincide with an opening for maximum receptivity and increased commitment to the coaching challenge.

As an example, if someone offered to provide you with a free public speaking coaching session today, would you make the appointment? Perhaps. Now let's say that the same person offered you a free coaching session on pubic speaking today and you had the most important speech of your life planned for tomorrow. Would you be more likely to make the appointment now? Of course. So an opening is a moment when the client finds coaching especially attractive or needed.

Coaching and the Creative Process

Christine Brown McCarthy, MBA, MSW

When I first started coaching Clare, she had been writing a novel during downtime at work and in spurts at home. She was eager to get it finished and published. She had spoken to other authors and agents, and at one level was convinced that she could create a work that would be meaningful to others and would be published. But the artist in her was full of self-doubt, self-consciousness, and uncertainty.

Clare is highly disciplined, has boundless energy, is very imaginative, and is easily able put her ideas into action. But she just could not seem to get the book finished. Coaching her was fascinating and challenging.

While I am sure we could have had a successful coaching relationship without it, I am convinced that real work began when she decided to let me read her manuscript and to share new chapters and revisions with me. Allowing me not only to read it but to comment on it and ask questions about it was a powerful yet extremely fragile gift that I handled with great care. It was an intimate act, one of great risk for her. I felt I had been entrusted not only with her work but also with her soul. As a result, it seemed as though we worked on two parallel planes, with our sessions ranging from the mundane to the ephemeral.

Her stated goal was to get the book finished as soon as possible. When I explored why this was so important, it boiled down to her wanting the money and wanting to be free to "pursue other things." My instincts told me this was part of the problem: writing had become a chore rather than the passion it once was.

At work she was typing the text directly into the computer. At home she was writing it in longhand and then entering it on the computer at work. Taking time to write at work was problematic because she had a high-level position and managed a large staff. When I asked what it would take to improve things, she said she needed a computer at home but couldn't afford one. I helped her arrange a way to borrow a laptop on the way home.

...continued on next page

We began to talk about the characters. I really wanted to get to know them. I began asking her questions about their speech patterns. I began asking why they behaved the way they did. It was fascinating to hear her responses and then see her come to the realization that she had not captured a lot of this on paper. I questioned the symbolism of some of the names. This was another area she was not conscious of.

Clare continued to focus on getting the book done. She complained that she did not have a place of her own to work. She shared that while in graduate school she wrote on an ironing board next to her bed and was having a hard time recreating the same setup in her home. We explored the reality of this. It came down to the layout of her bedroom and which side of the bed her husband slept on. Making changes here was not an option. Giving herself permission to take over the guest room and make it her own was a big step for her.

We talked about the use of quotation marks and indentation, about the proper spelling for names of trees, about the geography and descriptions of the landscape of the settings, and about class differences.

Clare was not able to control interruptions of her time. She was getting up at 4:30 a.m. to write. Her husband and son were self-sufficient in the morning, but she was answering the door when her neighbor dropped off her son at 5:45 a.m. to wait for the bus. In the evenings and on weekends she answered phone calls and got involved with neighbors who were taking advantage of her good nature and generosity in helping them with problems. She began to set and enforce stronger boundaries. She began to think of herself as a writer.

We talked about the historic events that engulfed the fictional characters and about her experiences at the time of the setting for the book. And mine. And how different they were. And yet I could identify with the characters. Perhaps there was a much larger theme to her book. We talked about what that might be.

Gradually the urgency of finishing the book receded and the passion returned. The characters deepened. The book got longer

...continued on next page

and richer. Clare was eager to go back and rewrite sections. She learned to take advantage of the word processing program she was using as she was editing it. She immersed herself in the process, not the product. She was enjoying herself again. She did finish the book, nearly a year past her self-imposed deadline, and was tremendously pleased with the book and herself. She is now working on her next book. It has not been published yet, and that's okay with her.

ACTION STEPS

Therapists transitioning to coaching must adjust from spending considerable time encouraging clients to elaborate more deeply on their trauma, pain, and the connections to past behaviors and feelings to spending more time helping clients develop action steps that over time move them significantly closer to their goals. If we think of progress toward a major life goal as a trail to the top of a mountain, action steps can be like hopping from one boulder to another: eventually enough steps and hops will get us to the top of the mountain.

To design action steps, first have clients focus on an important goal. Then ask them, "What are some of the smaller steps that you need to take to get to that goal?" or "See yourself having achieved that goal . . . When you look backwards, what were the steps you took to get to where you are now?"

Once clients identify the steps that need to be taken, have them write those down and then rank-order what steps would be most helpful to do first. Then have them identify actions they can take that are part of that step. Ask them to choose: "What are specific action steps you will take in the coming week and when are you going to do it?"

Sometimes in the interest of time you might "request" that your client take a particular action step. When making a request it is a good idea to give the client three choices: your client can agree with the request, decline your request, or make a counteroffer.[22] When clients decline a request, you can choose whether you want to explain the request more clearly, and with more supporting data, in case they didn't understand the reasoning behind it. Then ask, "So what aspects of this suggestion do seem to fit as a potential action, or if not, what is your counteroffer of what you will do?"

IDENTIFYING AND MANAGING OBSTACLES

A fundamental step in coaching is to help your clients identify potential obstacles and plan for them. Inner obstacles or outer challenges occasionally arise. If their life issues were so easy to manage, they wouldn't choose to come to you.

Early in the coaching relationship, explain that obstacles will occasionally arise at times as an indication that they are pushing into higher ground. (Coaches generally avoid the term "resistance" with their clients and use the word "obstacles.") When you are developing action plans with your clients, build in a tentative, corresponding plan to navigate around obstacles, and be prepared to engage in a creative process to help the client navigate any difficulties that do arise.

Help clients become aware of whether the obstacles are internal obstacles or outer challenges. Examples of outer challenges (which, of course, have an inner component) include such things as losing one's day job, competition, legal challenges, divorce, and illness in the family. Some examples of inner obstacles are procrastinating, lack of time management, lack of seriousness, fear of taking necessary steps, too little money, too much money, perfectionism, too many pans in the fire, not learning what one needs to learn, lack of focus, and dysfunctional patterns.

One way to help clients anticipate and manage inner obstacles and outer challenges is to have them complete a four-step process:

1. Make a list of potential inner obstacles and outer challenges.

2. Rate them as likely or unlikely.

3. For any likely obstacles, write two sentences about how to manage that obstacle.

4. Identify a support group and supportive processes which would help them navigate the obstacle.

When an obstacle does appear, support your clients with your confidence that they will be able to manage the situation and convey that you are by their side as they face their struggles bravely. Here are some other tips for assisting clients to manage obstacles without taking their problems over as your own:

- Accept that it is not your job to remove the obstacle.

- Utilize advice-giving sparingly.

- Leave the decisions to the client.

- Observe ways that the client stays stuck.

- Utilize questions to let the client set the agenda.

- Practice patience and wait for the client to find the best path for himself or herself.

- Have clients write down their vision. You are coaching clients to clarify their finest vision of how they want to be at the end of the coaching.

- Continue to ask your client about his or her vision, purpose, and goals. Clients' visions are a source of power to them.

- Learn how your client perceives the world, and think about how you can enrich that perception.

- Identify your client's "growing edge"—the words, actions, and images the client uses to deal with challenges constructively. Reinforce words and actions that reflect your client's growing edge to help the client move beyond obstacles.[23]

ACCOUNTABILITY TECHNIQUES

One of the most powerful elements of the coaching relationship is the accountability dynamic. As a coach, you help people move forward by encouraging their engagement in action toward purposeful, meaningful goals. Accountability is a major motivating factor that facilitates your clients' follow-through on their expressed commitments.

Three common questions promote accountability:

- "What are you planning on doing?"
- "When will you do this?"
- "How will I know you did it?"

The "what" question commits the client to a specific action. Asking "when" commits the client to a specific time to engage in the action. The follow-up question "How will I know you did it?" further structures the commitment by calling for a response such as "I'll send you an e-mail Friday morning." The potential difficulty of obstacles can be managed by rehearsal by asking, "What obstacles may arise that could interfere with you doing what you are saying you are going to do?" and "What is your plan to manage that potential obstacle?"

The coaching philosophy of focusing on the client's agenda enables the coach to ask the client the next week about the outcome of the agreed-to action steps. The client created his or her own agenda, so the coach's follow-up questions usually aren't perceived as nagging or confrontational.

The coaching concept of accountability is also a powerful tool for the client. The client gives an account of what happened. The accountability tool allows the client to clarify:

- What worked?

- What didn't work?

- What would I do differently next time?

What do you do when clients don't do what they said they were going to do? You can positively confront the client by saying, "I noticed you didn't send that e-mail, as you said you would. How do you want to handle being accountable in this relationship?"[24]

Accountability is an extremely powerful part of the coaching relationship, but don't let it be the whole relationship. Masterful coaches attempt to keep the coaching relationship open to other processes that complement accountability, such as values clarification, identification of purpose, and movement in developmental areas.

FORWARDING THE ACTION

"Forwarding the action" is coaching jargon for the coach's interventions that facilitate clients' committing to action steps to bring them closer to the stated outcomes of the coaching agenda. Facilitating a client's movement means using a broad array of coaching skills at the appropriate time. Examples of ways that coaches help clients move forward include the following:

- Inquiry: "What are two creative new ways you can help yourself move forward in the coming month?"

- Validating a client's unique idea: "This sounds like a dynamic new idea that taps into a powerful way that you can unleash your potential."

- Bottom-lining: "To clarify, what is the bottom line on the most important challenge you are facing this week?"

■ Action in the session: "How about we identify those factors right now in the session? What specifically is your projected gross income and your projected expenditures for the next six months?"

Forwarding the Action

Marcia Reynolds, M.A., M.Ed., MCC
Past President, International Coach Federation

My client was president of a distributor of pharmaceutical products in Phoenix, Arizona. His presenting challenges were (1) too much paperwork overflowing to his home office; (2) needing to bring his employees into alignment with company goals (few employees were taking initiative, resulting in too much work for him); (3) no time for himself, for exercise and self-care; and (4) not feeling as if he had much to look forward to for himself in the overall picture of his life.

In three months' time, the client made major shifts in his work and life in a number of areas.

1. How to set boundaries, at home and at work. After I asked the question "What would it take for you to feel clarity and calmness [two values he identified for himself] in your life?" the client listed situations in his personal life as well as some at work that were draining his energy. He felt he needed to be clear with what he needed, and how he should be treated by his ex-wife, children, and employees. Typically, as father and company president, he took on everyone's problems and was expected to fix everything at the expense of taking care of himself. The shift came when he realized he did not need to take care of everyone to be valued. He learned that he could actually be more effective by facilitating self-sufficiency. And by delegating work, he empowered those around him, personally and professionally.

2. Creating a vision with his employees so they will buy in to the direction of the company. This included sharing information on where he saw the company growing—such as

...continued on next page

including new product lines of vitamins and herbs—and how this information fit into the mission of helping to improve the quality of life of their customers. Once he shared this information, he asked his employees to describe their perfect day at work in the future, when they hit the financial goals he had outlined. The employees then read their personal visions out loud in small groups. From there, they looked at similarities and discussed what was most important to them in the workplace. At the end of the day, each group presented action steps detailing how they would work together to reach the company's goals relating to the three identified areas of sales, internal communications, and work processes.

3. Scheduling "fun time" for himself, as well as time to read and meditate. First, the client had to define what "fun" was to him beyond work. As he determined what brought him joy, some of the items were things other people might define as "work," such as preparing his small estate for landscaping. His list also included activities he had long since given up, such as playing the guitar. Fun has now become a scheduled event, not something to think about only if there is time.

4. Cleaning his personal spaces so he didn't feel so overwhelmed. The client dedicated time to organizing his offices (at work and at home) so he had more energy to deal with his day. He also looked at areas of his work that he could let go of and delegate to his managers.

5. Expanding his circle of friends for support and recreation, and creating a vision for his own life so he feels that he has something to look forward to. After working on his own vision, the client found he actually had much to look forward to. With the clearing of energy and space, he found more time to work on new ideas for his business, including the new product lines, a website, and more international business. Work still gets overwhelming at times, but he is much more capable of dealing with it. In a session that marked the end of the third month of coaching, he told me, "Balance doesn't have to do with how you spend your time. It has to do with how you feel about how you're spending your time."

CONCLUDING THE COACHING RELATIONSHIP

As the coaching moves toward concluding, you are engaging in two important processes: (1) validating and empowering the client and (2) providing an appropriate "ritual" to create a feeling of closure and yet leave the door open for more coaching.

Near the end of the coaching relationship, the focus is often on such things as the following:

- rehearsing the plans
- discussing the vision
- providing feedback and different perspectives to the client
- celebrating and validating the client's progress
- acknowledging the effort required and inevitable challenges in the future
- creating a follow-up schedule of phone coaching support for a few months, once or twice a month
- perhaps scheduling six-month and one-year follow-up coaching appointments
- saying thank you and good-bye
- acknowledging that the relationship will change

Often clients who have been in long-term coaching relationships may ask if they can arrange the option of calling you in the future for just a few sessions to follow up if the need arises. Sometimes you will find it helpful to arrange a planned phasing-out of the formal coaching relationship, for example shifting to a once-a-month meeting for three to six months as a concluding transition. This type of coaching may focus on

- successes and celebrations

- challenges or disappointments

- changes suggested to the client's strategic plan because of new external or internal conditions and situations

If you haven't talked with the client for a long time, the client may experience pressure in wanting to cover an unrealistic number of topics, so it is helpful to establish a clear focus early. Thus, you might ask, "What will be the focus, or goal, that you have for this coaching call?" When the coaching really feels like it has come to a full conclusion, a wonderful way to conclude is to suggest that you each write a letter to the other expressing gratitude and recognition.

SUMMARY

Effective coaching requires a combination of a mature, well-balanced individual, who is high in emotional intelligence and is continually learning the art and practice of effective coaching. In this chapter, seventeen techniques or coaching mindsets were presented as well as five illustrative vignettes. Some of these tools and mental models you will be able to integrate immediately, while others will require you to have additional formal coach training, to be observed, and to be given feedback by experienced coaches—and of course, you will need to accumulate adequate experience with these techniques.

CHAPTER 7

Assessment in Coaching

Therapists, who usually have some training in the use of assessments, and especially those who have been using assessments in their clinical practice, will find it valuable to incorporate them into coaching. The skilled use of assessments is clearly a way for graduate-level professionals to bring an empirically validated, value-enhancing tool to the coaching arena. Assessments can help the coach quickly learn about the clients personality, preferred interaction style, attitudes and values.

Most of the assessments described in this chapter require that the coach meet the particular educational requirements of the respective test manufacturer. Usually this means having a graduate degree in a field that provides training in the use of psychological tests. Coaches should use assessments as but one component of an integrated assessment process in order to develop a coaching agenda. Other important components are a direct interview and observation of the client, and possibly feedback reports from others. In accordance with the test manufacturers' recommendations and the American Psychological Association, reasonable care should be undertaken to ensure that the testing materials themselves remain secure. Moreover, the assessment results should be treated as confidential.

An exciting new development for coaches conducting their work over the telephone is that some test distributors have their assessments available online. This is a convenient, efficient method for you to be able to deliver a useful service to your clients without you having to ask your clients to come to your office for test administration or for you to travel to their site. The disadvantage of mailing the instruments is that APA and test manufacturer's guidelines usually state that you should not let your clients take the actual assessments home with them to prevent unauthorized copying which could eventually diminish reliability.

This chapter describes four of the prominent assessment tools used in the coaching field. There are many other quality instruments, and their absence here is not meant to suggest that they are any less valuable than those included.

MYERS-BRIGGS TYPE INDICATOR (MBTI)

The most widely used assessment tool in coaching conducted by individuals with graduate degrees in psychology is the Myers-Briggs Type Indicator® (MBTI®). The MBTI, based on Isabel Myers's interpretation of Jung's theory of psychological type, has been in use for over fifty years. The MBTI is widely used to help individuals explore how their "preferences" relate to career "fit." It is used by couples to help them understand differences as natural inclinations and strengths rather than as faults, and it is used in industry to help create teams with a diversity of strengths and to help team members value their differences. It is estimated that over two million people a year take the MBTI instrument.

There are many versions of the MBTI that are available to the graduate-level practitioner. I recommend that you use the Step II, Form K, Expanded Interpretive Report, if you are new to the instrument. You receive a twenty-four-page report with enough detail to make the information highly personalized and useful to your client, and written in an explanatory style that allows you to give the complete report to your client after you review it with them. The MBTI Step II, Form K consists of 131 items and takes thirty-five minutes to complete.

The MBTI instrument helps clients understand their "preferences" on four scales: Extraversion-Introversion, Sensing-Intuition, Thinking-Feeling, and Judging-Perceiving. The unique preferences of the client are combined to illuminate one of sixteen personality types.

Individuals find that personality preference information can help them have more direction in their lives by helping them understand that they have tendencies for certain styles of thinking and interacting. As an assessment tool in coaching, the MBTI can give coaches insights into which coaching approaches to life challenges are going to complement a client's strengths. The coach can also use the MBTI to help clients understand the strengths of their preferences. Knowing their strengths can aid clients in planning personal and career decisions. Many of my coaching clients are entrepreneurs, and I have found that identifying their type with the MBTI helps the coaching process to maximize the use of their strengths in their business efforts. In *Joining the Entrepreneurial Elite: Four Styles to Business Success*, Olaf Isachsen describes how to relate personality type, which you identify with the MBTI, to entrepreneurial style.[1]

Keep in mind that personality type, properly utilized, or any other single assessment result, never puts people in a box and never explains all aspects of a person's personality or behavior. There are endless nuances to an individual's personality. The four styles that Isachsen describes are presented here to give you an idea of how personality type can provide a preliminary indication of what type of coaching style may fit for a particular client. Then the coach will rely on conversation with the client and observation of the client's behavior to help guide the coach's approach. Isachsen's four styles are Administrator, Tactician, Strategist, and Idealist.

Clients with an Administrator style of entrepreneurship are excellent at accomplishing what they set out to do. They achieve goals in an orderly manner and on time. Through coaching they can learn that they need to balance their orderliness with an emphasis on keeping customers and employees satisfied and loyal. An Administrator is a "sensing-judging" person on the Myers-Briggs assessment.

A Tactician's style is extremely energetic. Tacticians are not prone to contemplate, but instead are energized by achievement. They instinctively know what action to take. They are highly flexible and focus on what needs to be done right now. They often take the greatest risks of all the entrepreneurs. Coaching can benefit Tacticians by giving them a structured forum to discuss the long-term view of their business, something they are unlikely to do on their own. A Tactician is a "sensing perceiver" on the Myers-Briggs assessment.

Strategists are highly self-sufficient people who have a clear view of the future. They focus on "what to be" and move steadily toward their goals. Rather than settle for what they have already achieved, they keep striving for higher standards. The coaching process can help Strategists take into account the importance of considering other team members' feelings to improve their organization's effectiveness. A Strategist is an "intuitive thinker" on the Myers-Briggs assessment.

Idealists are authentic and warm with others while maintaining a persistent focus on their cause and the people on their team. Idealists are dreamers and usually find failure unacceptable. Idealist entrepreneurs are gifted at bringing out the best in people and can often be very persuasive. Coaches can help Idealists put a foundation under their business dreams through realistic planning and follow-through. An Idealist is an "intuitive feeler" on the Myers-Briggs assessment.

CALIFORNIA PSYCHOLOGICAL INVENTORY (CPI)

Assessments such as the California Psychological Inventory™ (CPI), which usually are used by psychologist coaches, can provide dynamic objective information about personality and behavior, as well as an indication of whether a client is appropriate for coaching or psychotherapy. (A shortened version of the CPI is planned that will be available for purchase by individuals with a master's degree and appropriate training.) Such an assessment can help give the coach quicker insight into a client's interpersonal style, social expertise, personal interests, values, and achievement orientation. Insight into these elements of the client's personality can help the coach understand the client's motivation and what approaches might fit best with that individual.

The CPI consists of 434 items and takes fifty minutes to complete. The inventory indicates a range of ego integration—from self-fulfilled, superior ego integration to dispirited, poor ego integration, with low realization of a positive potential. In the case of a dispirited, poorly integrated individual, the CPI can be useful to help determine that a client is more appropriate for an in-office, therapeutic relationship than for coaching.

The CPI's twenty folk scales measure social expertise, interpersonal style, maturity, achievement orientation, and personal styles. Although not specifically designed for this purpose, these scales can be of assistance when assessing a client before and after the implementation of a developmental coaching plan.

FIRO-B (FUNDAMENTAL INTERPERSONAL RELATIONS ORIENTATION-BEHAVIOR)

The FIRO-B™ (Fundamental Interpersonal Relations Orientation-Behavior™) is a useful tool to understand how clients' personal needs affect their behavior toward other people. The FIRO-B consists of 54 items and takes fifteen minutes to complete.

This interesting instrument, widely used in leadership development and management, provides insight into clients' needs for inclusion, control, and affection. Understanding a client's need for inclusion will help you understand how much "contact" a client seeks from others and how much contact the client wants to give. Learning about your client's need for control helps you understand how much power or dominance the client exudes to others and how much control the client desires to be directed toward them. Insight into your client's need for affection provides insight into how much "closeness" the client extends to others and desires from others.

The FIRO-B also provides information on your client's compatibility with others, so it is especially helpful when designing coaching plans related to relationship issues, management and executive development, and team building. See the Chapter 7 endnotes (note 2) for information on where to obtain the MBTI, CPI, and FIRO-B assessments.

Assessment and Coaching

Ana Maria Montes, Ph.D., MPEC

Background Information

Scott Fisher is in his middle forties. He is a family man and a regional executive for a service company at the national level.

Scott sees himself as hardworking and honest but knows that he has some problems in his leadership. He has received feedback that he is seen as a person who is hard to work for. He hopes that coaching can help him be more accessible and personable to his direct reports, less rigid, and easier going.

Scott completed a number of assessments, including the Myers-Briggs Type Indicator® (MBTI) and the Fundamental Interpersonal Relations Orientation-Behavior (FIRO-B). Here I describe the use of these two assessments with Scott.

MBTI Results and Application

Scott's MBTI is INTJ (Introverted Intuition with Thinking). INTJs are generally Strategists.[3] They are seen as

- original thinkers

- interested and innovative

- having single-minded concentration

- unimpressed with authority

- naturally high achievers

...continued on next page

Their strengths are to be

- pragmatic
- conceptual
- tenacious
- analytical

Their opportunities for growth are

- being sensitive to others' needs
- taking care of routine details
- learning to yield to others' points
- taking time to smell the roses
- trying to be more empathic in relationships

They are frustrated by

- routine
- redundancy
- being sidetracked by other's needs and opinions
- being told what do or how to do things

They irritate others by

- refusing to yield
- being overtly demanding or insistent on having their own way

...continued on next page

- arrogance

- skepticism

- hair-splitting

- moving too fast

- lack of execution

They value

- logic

- ideas

- ingenuity

On a team:

- they analyze the alternatives

INTJs' quest:

- Competence

INTJs' Achilles heel:

- Incompetence

I presented this information about common qualities of many INTJs to Scott along with information about other personality styles. The scores were presented by telling Scott, "People with this type of profile generally are . . . How does this fit you?" In order for Scott to see his uniqueness, and the uniqueness of others,

...continued on next page

I asked him the following coaching questions:

- In looking at your style, how similar or different do you think you are from your boss?

- What do you think are the styles of those direct reports that you are having the most difficulty communicating with?

- How do you like others to communicate with you?

- Do you think that you are giving others the style of communication that is the most effective for them?

- What yardstick are you using to evaluate others?

- Do you have the same expectations for others as you have for yourself?

- Do others have the same level of knowledge that you do?

Scott's responses indicated that his boss was an even more exaggerated version of himself. He could see the problems that this brought for others. He was also able to see that the people that he had the most difficulty with were those that in his view were the most dissimilar to himself. He acknowledged that his style of communication was perhaps not the most effective way of communicating.

Scott admitted that he did want others to measure up to his own expectations. The dialogue clarified that it was not an issue of having low or high expectations. I encouraged him to have high expectations of his direct reports, but to set stretch goals that were in accordance with their capabilities and not necessarily with his own.

Scott also became cognizant that he did not take the time to see whether his direct reports had clearly understood what he expected from them. He thought that the suggestion of having each one summarize their specific responsibilities at the end of a meeting would help make sure that there were no gaps between what he said and what they understood. This would help reduce

...continued on next page

how critical he became when people did not do what he thought they were supposed to do. `

FIRO-B Results and Application

Scott's FIRO-B scores were as follows:

Expressed:
    Inclusion: 4   Control: 8   Affection: 5

Wanted:
    Inclusion: 0   Control: 4   Affection: 5

Scott's FIRO-B inclusion scores were in the range of a moderate expressed inclusion need and a low wanted inclusion need. This score range generally indicates that people are social but do not have the need for constant socialization. They maintain an exclusive club of people they accept. They like to work in teams that allow the individual to follow through independently. Often they engage in social activities only if they think doing so will be productive.

Scott's FIRO-B control scores were in the range of a high expressed need for control and a moderate wanted control from others. This range of scores generally indicates comfort with making and assuming many responsibilities. It is usually difficult for people with this profile to sit back and let others take over. Most likely they set very high goals for themselves and want to feel they are excelling. Usually they want to have a say about how things will be done. There is a tendency not to delegate or to let others make their own decisions, a style that might hinder others' development and growth.

Scott's FIRO-B affection scores were in the range of a moderate expressed need for affection and a moderate wanted need for affection. This generally indicates someone who is comfortable both in showing warmth and in receiving it, although extreme demonstrations of closeness or coolness may make the person uncomfortable.

...continued on next page

I shared this information with Scott. These are some of the questions I asked him:

- What are some of your thoughts about this information? How does it seem to fit, and what ideas does it bring up for you?

- If you agree that you may have a relatively low need to socialize, how does that relate to not wanting to be involved in social activities unless you have to be for the benefit of the organization?

- What kind of unintended message do you think your socialization patterns might give to others?

- What relationship do you see between your high need to be in control and your demand for competence combined with the feedback you've gotten that you are a hard person to work for?

- Your affection scores and your comments indicate that you care about your direct reports. Do you think you communicate that to them? How?

- What messages do you think they get when you take away a task because they are not doing it the way you want?

- Given that you emphasize logic and data, how are you including the human element as a variable in the equation? Or do you see it as external to the bottom line or end results?

- Given that your expressed inclusion shows that you see value in initiating social interactions, how do you think that you could extend the amount and diversity of those interactions? Could you see more of those social interactions as investments rather than as chit chatting or socializing with no specific purpose?

...continued on next page

- Do you believe that you are more critical when you are under stress?

- Do you see that by remaining in control and taking more and more responsibilities, you are placing yourself under chronic stress?

- What can you do to reduce your stress?

- What can you delegate?

- What can help you delegate?

The dialogue and these types of questions allowed Scott to take a better look at himself and to understand the impact he was having on others. He also was able to set a plan of action to help him achieve his goals. I also suggested two popular self-help books that related to his interests.

Scott's developmental plan included the following elements:

- including the impact on others as a variable in his decision making

- summarizing with his direct reports and others what each one would do, to ensure that everyone was on the same page

- making a systematic effort to socialize with all his reports, including calendaring these activities

- meeting with each report to determine his or her developmental goals

- beginning to delegate to direct reports according to their developmental goals

MULTI-RATER FEEDBACK ASSESSMENTS

Multi-rater-feedback instruments, also called 360-degree feedback, provide information about an individual from all directions: self-report and feedback from supervisors, peers, and direct reports. These tools are used extensively in large companies, with the international business community spending billions of dollars to enhance performance. Two popular multi-rater feedback instruments (there are more than thirty different tools available) with high validity are the Benchmarks and the Campbell Leadership Index.[4] When clients receive anonymous feedback from several people, they have powerful information that can help clients shape the coaching agenda and the developmental plan. Most commonly, multi-rater feedback instruments are used to discern what behaviors the client is demonstrating that are linked to success and what behaviors could be improved to further career effectiveness. In particular, these instruments can be used to help the client

- develop greater self-awareness
- see how others perceive him or her
- make connections between behaviors and the perceptions of others
- examine how the client relates to people in authority, to those in similar positions, and to those who work under the client
- set goals
- plan to overcome misperceptions or problem behaviors that could derail the client's career
- reinforce and build on client strengths

Leaders in the organizational psychology field have urged additional research into how best to gather and use multi-rater feedback.[5] This is partly because the quick adoption of these feedback tools has not allowed time for people to investigate how best to incorporate these tools into a coaching program. In Fortune 500 companies that use these feedback instruments heavily, some have complained that they result in a paper jungle and that the results aren't used effectively. The increasing number of coaches with advanced training in psychology can be of special value in furthering a more scientific approach to 360-degree feedback in the corporate world.

SUMMARY

Mental health professional coaches have several exclusive assessment instruments that are not available for general public purchase. Once you are trained in and have experience using these assessment instruments, you will have added a powerful, value-added component to coaching. In this chapter we have reviewed how commonly used assessments are incorporated into coaching. The vignette provided by Dr. Montes demonstrates how assessment results are incorporated into a powerful feedback coaching session. Most importantly, coaches can utilize assessments to help clients identify and develop their strengths, discover how others perceive their behavior and performance, and recognize and manage blindspots and developmental needs. Moreover, competent coaches recognize that assessments are just one tool, albeit a powerful one, in the coach's toolkit.

PART THREE

Varieties of Coaching

❖ ❖ ❖

Coaching Transitions and Facilitating Strategic Life Plans

CHAPTER 8

C arl Jung proposed the idea that individuals travel through a "life cycle." Jung coined the term "individuation" to represent the developmental process that adults move through. He particularly emphasized that much of adult development begins in the second half of life, the "noon of life."[1]

Coaches are increasingly being called to help already successful people navigate the challenges and dreams that arise through adult development. This chapter describes two common coaching situations: helping people navigate a life transition and facilitating a strategic life plan.

LIFE TRANSITIONS

In Chapter 1, I introduced Frederic Hudson's account of "life chapters" and "life transitions."[2] Throughout life, people are either in one or the other. The cycle of moving from life chapter to life transition and then on to a new life chapter is repeated over and over.

Identifying Where Clients Are in the Life Chapter/Transition Cycle

Frederic Hudson emphasizes the importance of understanding what phase of life a client is in. According to Hudson, in phase one of a life chapter, people experience a period of success and stability. They commit to goals and move forward to success. Their modus operandi is to "go for it!" During this phase, coaches help clients formulate their goals, support them, and hold them accountable for moving forward. Often clients experience excitement, the thrill of finding their passion, and the joy of meeting a challenge. At the same time, they may feel extremely busy, stressed, or competitive. They may need support to let go of extraneous involvements so they can be more effective in career and family life; to acquire new skills; to network well; and to take time for nurturing their souls during a busy stage.

In phase two of a life chapter, people often experience boredom and restlessness. They may feel irritable, dissatisfied, or disenchanted. Some people may ask, "Is this all there is?" In terms of career, for example, perhaps their industry or company is changing in ways that are difficult to adapt to, or perhaps they feel like they have "been there, done that" and thirst for something new. Phase two of a life chapter ends with either a mini-transition or a life transition.

A mini-transition is a kind of tune-up of one's existing life. A life transition is a longer, deeper reflective process of seeking a substantially new direction, often with a new understanding of the meaning of one's life. Whereas a mini-transition might involve moving to a different city or changing jobs within the same industry, a life transition may result in a substantial lifestyle change, a complete career change, or a decision to end a marriage.

In *Transitions: Making Sense of Life's Changes,* William Bridges writes that transitions are characterized by a feeling of something important ending, a period of confusion and distress, and a new beginning.[3] Categories of transitions include the loss of a relationship, changes in home life, beginning a new relationship, change in health, career and financial changes, and inner changes such as new, emerging values or new perspectives. Unlike the frequently positive feelings of challenge and excitement associated with a life chapter, the emotions people may experience during a transition can be not only strong but also painful. They may experience anger, sadness, frustration, a feeling of being stuck or trapped, resentment, and fear.

Coaching Clients in Transition

One of the most common reasons that people seek out coaches is to get help designing an exit plan from an outdated situation and navigating a mini-transition or a life transition. Coaches can assist clients to create a viable exit plan, reconnect with friends, explore a new job or career, obtain training or therapy, and develop an effective support network. They can mentor clients, motivate them, help them develop transition plans that will increase their self-confidence, assist them to develop strategies to overcome barriers, and help them problem-solve.

To illustrate the process of coaching transitions, let's consider the example of career transitions. As a coach, you can help clients in many ways as they navigate career transitions. For example, after assessing a client's current situation and preferences, you can help the client explore possible career paths and coach the person to follow a career path that blends with his or her unique preferences and personality. You can then help the client identify the specific steps that need to be taken to accomplish the career change, and you can support the client through the process of taking these steps and overcoming obstacles that arise along the way.

Begin with assessment. You can help a client evaluate whether his or her current job is a good fit by asking questions such as these:

- "Are you energized by your work?"
- "Do you feel appreciated for your work?"
- "Are you proud when you describe your work to others?"
- "Do you enjoy the people you work with?"
- "Do you feel hopeful about your career future?"
- "Do you enjoy your work?"

More broadly, the following are examples of coaching questions related to career development and transitions that you could pose to clients. (Many of these questions were inspired by Richard Bolles's *What Color Is Your Parachute?*).[4]

- "What challenges do you have in your career?"

- "What lessons have you learned in your work and what lesson do you think you are in the process of learning now?"

- "What assessment tools or questionnaires would you like to take?"

- "What books or tapes have you wanted to learn from that you haven't read or listened to yet?"

- "What are your strengths and weaknesses related to your current job?"

- "What is your most urgent development need for your current or upcoming job role?"

- "What are your favorite kinds of things to work with?" *Examples:* Computers, art supplies, books, journals, financial information, plants.

- "What is your favorite form of information to work with?" *Examples:* Books, journals, workshops, formal classes, audiotapes.

- "What do you like to use information for?" *Examples:* Make recommendations, make goals, develop solutions, audit systems, describe and research.

- "What are your favorite people to work with?" *Examples:* Men primarily, women primarily, no difference between genders, children, adolescents, young adults, people in their thirties, middle-aged people, seniors, retired people, people of a particular faith, people of a particular educational background.

- "What issues do you like to help people with?" *Examples:* Education, handicaps, pain, career challenge, stress, financial planning, values, marriage, spirituality, life planning.

- "What rewards do you want from your career?" *Examples:* A certain salary level, to be a member of a

> team, to be the boss, to have a chance to help others, to be creative, to be able to use all my skills, to be appreciated by others, to help others spiritually, intellectual stimulation, a flexible work schedule, to make a vision come true, to make things better, to learn and grow, to leave a legacy.

After clients have responded to questions like these, you might suggest this exercise to them:

> *Looking over your answers, write one paragraph summarizing what you have learned about your preferences related to work.*

Traditionally career counseling has included helping people look at their abilities, interests, and values. In addition to questions like the ones listed above, coaches can go further in helping clients move forward with career transition issues by helping them understand their personality type. The better a career matches a client's personality type, the more satisfied the client will be with his or her job. In this connection, coaches may find assessments and reports like the Myers-Briggs Type Indicator®, the Strong Interest Inventory®, and the MBTI® Career Report useful to provide a foundation for career transition coaching.[5]

When clients feel that a change in career is indicated, career transition coaching can help them move to the action phase. You can help clients prepare themselves for new career options by updating to new knowledge, acquiring new skills, clarifying performance expectations, and finding the "learning laboratories" necessary to successfully prepare for a transition.

For example, you can coach your clients in

- skill building to facilitate a promotion or a career transition

- performance improvement in particular areas to earn the recognition, or the self-confidence, to facilitate a promotion or a transition to a new career option

- developing themselves in ways that prepare them for a career transition or promotion

- creating a personal career agenda by exploring their ideal careers and the steps needed to reach their destination

In summary, coaching clients through transitions—whether career-related or otherwise—involves assessing and probing the current situation, helping the client envision new possibilities, exploring these possibilities in the light of a client's dreams and values, helping the client chart a course for change that includes necessary steps, and supporting the client in the implementation of the change plan. The sample questions presented in the previous section are an example of coaching questions related to career transitions. However, they can easily be adapted to other types of transitions by swapping out the "career" focus and substituting the other, relevant transition subject for your client. Simply by letting clients know that transitions·—and the uncomfortable feelings associated with them—are normal events in life, coaches can encourage clients to take the plunge into constructive change. Beyond this initial support, specific coaching on the action steps the client needs to take can empower them to successfully navigate a life transition.

Helping a Client Make a Career Transition

Barbara Doyle, M.A.

Several years ago, Bill, a man in his early forties, requested professional coaching for a career transition. Bill was a licensed architect who had just been let go from a position with a mid-sized architectural firm. Bill told me that he needed help to evaluate where he was and what he wanted to do.

At this time it was necessary to clarify Bill's goals, assess his situation, and support his decisions. We established that Bill wanted to remain in the field of architecture but would instead prefer to work for a real estate firm rather than an architectural firm in the position of project manager or development director.

Bill had excellent networking connections and many resources. We discussed at length how to contact his network of referral resources and build on his many relationships. I encouraged him to make as many inquiries as possible in one week. Bill's internal commitment to making this transition allowed him to follow through on the plan we had developed.

A former employer offered Bill a position in his architectural firm. We discussed that this was an employer that knew him and that he enjoyed working for, but on the down side it was a step backward and it wasn't what he really wanted to do. After discussing the pros and cons of accepting this position, Bill decided that this would be a source of income for him and his family and that he would accept this position. In the interim he would continue to work on finding the position he wanted.

Although his time was limited, now that Bill had a full-time position he still remained accountable as he developed a new action plan based on his goals for the future. In one of our coaching sessions, Bill and I brainstormed some options he had in his profession. He mentioned working as a consultant rather than an employee. He liked the idea that it was entrepreneurial and that he would be in business for himself, but he also worried about the work drying up and that it might not be permanent. He decided to contact real estate developers and propose that he

...continued on next page

work for them in a consulting capacity. He quickly received a contract to manage a remodeling project on a consulting basis from a large developer who owned major shopping malls.

Again this was not exactly what he wanted, but Bill decided that it was in the area that he desired and that he did not want to pass it by. This was not an easy decision because being in business for himself was not at all what he had first envisioned. It was at this time that Bill needed to adjust his thinking and challenge his former commitment. We looked at the ramifications of the decision he faced. I asked, "What would be different in your life, what additional commitments would you be taking on, what obstacles might arise, and based on these conclusions, what would be an appropriate course of action?"

I worked with Bill over a course of several years. His commitment to change and his continued ability to optimize his resources allowed him to grow both personally and professionally. Bill worked as an independent consultant for two years. The decision turned out to be very lucrative and served as a stepping stone into his next transition.

FACILITATING STRATEGIC LIFE PLANS

Coaches help clients discover what they are most passionate about, most committed to, and what activities and styles are most in line with their strengths. Then they help clients combine passion, commitment, and strengths into a compelling purpose for their stage of life. Strategic life plan coaching involves transforming purpose into a vision and then converting the vision into a realistic plan through thoughtful, step-by-step actions. Adopting and working a strategic life plan can lead many clients to a life they thought could exist only in their dreams.

The steps to developing a strategic life plan include the following:

■ Know your personality.

- Know your values.

- Know your strengths.

- Know your passions.

- Find your purpose.

- Develop a vision.

- Create your plan.

Personality Type and Life Planning

Whether you are developing your own life plan or assisting your clients in developing theirs, I think it is helpful to have a conceptualization of your own personality as well as your client's. Coaches who understand their own personality type and preferences have a high degree of self-awareness. Self-awareness in turn allows coaches to recognize where they have to consciously adjust their coaching style away from what may come most naturally to them, to what is most helpful for their clients. This understanding will guide you in your coaching approach with your client. Understanding your client's personality type will better equip you in coaching your clients about the choices they are making in their life direction, especially in terms of how their choices fit well with their personality preferences and their strengths.

To examine personality preferences, I recommend using a personality assessment such as the Myers-Briggs Type Indicator® (MBTI)[6] or spending focused time helping your clients analyze what they prefer, how they prefer to act, and what they try to avoid. If you do use the MBTI or other instrument, recognize that no assessment tool can completely capture the uniqueness of a human being, so carefully analyze the results as "food for thought." Coaching that increases the client's understanding of his or her own personality can provide useful guidance in life by providing another source of information to aid in decision making.

Clients need to be educated that each personality type has unique strengths. We identify our personality types to understand our strengths, manage potential difficulties, and help us to appreciate others who are different from us.

As discussed in Chapter 7, the use of assessments provides much useful and specific information that after validation through discussion with the client will aid in the coaching process. If you are not using a formal assessment tool such as the MBTI, here are some general questions to ask yourself regarding a client's personality that touch on similar themes to the MBTI:

- Is the client more extroverted or introverted?

- Does the client gather information usually by focusing on the tangible and concrete? This preference would be focused on "senses."

- Does the client usually gather information by an abstract process, often patiently waiting for future rewards of his or her thought processes?

- Does the client tend to process information by focusing on feelings or on thoughts?

- Does the client tend to be structured when dealing with information, or more open and unstructured?

As I discussed in Chapter 7, Olaf Isachsen describes four personality styles of entrepreneurs: the Administrator, the Tactician, the Strategist, and the Idealist.[7] These styles can be related to many of the clients who come for coaching, since we are all entrepreneurs when we are creating a strategic plan for a life chapter. An understanding of these four styles will help you see more clearly your client's area of strengths as well as areas where coaching may be extra important.

Adapting these ideas to strategic life planning, we could say that the Administrator is someone who is down-to-earth, conscientious, and values stability. Administrators enjoy making a contribution and being recognized for their efforts. They are traditionalists who judge ideas for their fit with established practices and who tend to worry and protect themselves by being prepared for the worst. Administrators tend to be skeptical of new ideas and prefer to live in the world of proven arrangements. They value steady, dependable progress and appreciate others easily. This is a sensing-judging profile on the MBTI assessment.

The Tactician is quick to sense opportunities and puts a high value on freedom, which facilitates rapid decisions and action. Tacticians often feel stifled and frustrated in a large organization. They tend to live aggressively and don't worry about saving for a rainy day. Tacticians can be playful and can respond quickly and confidently in a crisis. They can become very focused on a goal and show little concern about creature comforts. Tacticians may not take the time to think things through well because exploring concepts isn't their preference. This is a sensing-perceiving profile on the MBTI assessment.

The Strategist tends to be independent, intuitive, highly optimistic, and focused on the future and on his or her own thoughts. Strategists love an intellectual challenge and work hard at everything they do. They can get bored when they have learned the answers, and some people might find them arrogant. Strategists mean no harm; it is just that other people's feelings are not their focus. This is an intuitive-thinker profile on the MBTI assessment.

The Idealist is motivated by a love of bringing people together. Idealists are energized more by people than by money. Often they are mentors who have great patience and sense of integrity. Idealists can create fantastic dreams and can bring people together to help realize them because they admire the authenticity of the person. To be successful, idealists can often benefit from encouragement to take more concrete action. This is an intuitive-feeler profile on the MBTI assessment.

Your understanding of the entrepreneurial style of your clients can help you and your clients in the development of strategic life plans that fit with their dominant approach to living.

Exploring Values, Strengths, and Passions

Facilitating a values-clarification process and an exploration of a client's strengths and passions can help prepare a solid foundation for a strategic life plan. The discussion in Chapter 6 about how to conduct a values- clarification process and the values-clarification exercise in the Appendix are valuable components to the creation of the bedrock of the strategic life plan.

Developing Purpose, Vision, and a Plan

People need three elements to create their ideal life: a purpose, a vision, and a plan. In *Life Launch*, Frederic Hudson and Pamela McLean illuminated the process and technique of discovering personal purpose, creating a vision or dream, and working a plan:

> *Purpose is a profound commitment to a compelling expectation for this time in your life ...*
>
> *Your purpose distills into a vision or dream, which is more precise and clear than your purpose, but less precise and clear than your plan ...*
>
> *The dream comes first. Reality chases after the dream, to make it happen ...*
>
> *To create a future, the dream must become a plan, as the dreamer becomes a planner.*[8]

Our purpose and vision are transformed into reality by planning. Planning is logical and detailed, and it has a time line. Strategic life planning is the conversion of purpose and vision into a step-by-step process of achieving one's dreams.

Sometimes clients feel paralyzed at the thought of trying to identify their purpose, vision, and plan because they think the coach means developing these for their whole life. Herein lies the beauty of describing Hudson's "life chapter" concept. Your clients will feel much more empowered and free to dream and plan if they understand that they are talking about the next several years—not the rest of their lives.

Here is a useful exercise that is important to do yourself before you ask your clients to do it. By this process you will experience the advantages yourself of engaging in focused, creative life planning. Do the following exercise now, or take out your calendar and schedule twenty minutes for this purpose to help you tap your ideas about how you want your life to be.

Ideal Vision Imagery Exercise

To help your clients creatively tap their inner wisdom about what they most want out of their life, adapt the following imagery exercise to your style of conducting imagery exercises and your client's preferences:

I'm curious about what your inner mind will reveal to you about your ideal vision of your emerging life chapter. Go ahead and enjoy and wonder what you will learn about your own ideal vision. Go to a favorite quiet spot to have some alone time without any interruptions. Perhaps you will take a walk to a quiet spot, sit at the beach, or have a quiet time at your home or office.

Allow yourself to relax and dream that you are living one year from now and that you are well on your way to creating your ideal life.

- *Encourage yourself to dream to tap into the power of your heart.*
- *What do you most enjoy doing?*
- *How do you use your time?*
- *What is the shape of your career?*
- *What is your business like? What are your work hours?*

- *How much money do you make? What are your revenue streams?*

- *What people do you want in your life? How do you want to be relating to them?*

- *What are the qualities of your personal life?*

- *What feelings and thoughts do you have now?*

- *Write down your vision and feelings to honor your inner guidance.*

Sample Ideas and Questions for Strategic Life Plan Development

The following are examples of coaching ideas and questions for helping clients develop a strategic life plan. These ideas are adapted from Hudson's LifeLaunch model, which is a popular and powerful three-day residential seminar.

As a coach, you will need to make the following suggestions "come alive" through invigorating, sincere conversation, curiosity, and commitment to the client. These ideas and questions are presented as "bare bones" and need to be adapted to the context of your relationship with your client. The process described may take weeks or months.

To begin, encourage your client to reflect on the values-clarification work that you did together early in the process. Then ask the client to complete this sentence:

"My purpose for the next several years is ..."

Explain that "your values, energy, and destination follow your purpose. Your purpose is your personal path, your calling." Hudson says the client's purpose is a sense of "destiny . . . an unstoppable drive."

Then ask your client to do a homework inquiry:

"Would you write a one- to two-paragraph vision of your ideal life or career for the next several years—a brief story of how you want your life to be? Don't be humble—let your passion through."

Once the vision has been articulated, help your client convert his or her dreams into a realistic plan by posing questions like the following:

- *"What activities do you want or need to do more of?"*
- *"What activities do you need to reduce or stop?"*
- *"What training would be helpful for you to engage in?"*
- *"What connections or networks would be attractive to create or join?"*
- *"What are the key steps involved in creating your ideal life?"*
- *"What are the approximate dates that those steps will be accomplished?"*
- *"What are two or three action items for each step that you've identified?"*

Finally, ask your client to sum up the plan in writing:

"Write a half-page preliminary strategy about how your passions, values, and strengths will lead you to your ideal destination in the next couple of years."

This powerful process of transforming vision and purpose into destiny is a rich, exciting path. Implementing a strategic life plan takes determination, focus, commitment, drive, passion, and the chutzpah to thing big. In the words of Anais Nin, "Life shrinks or expands in proportion to one's courage."

SUMMARY

Coaches are used increasingly to help already successful people move from one chapter of their lives to another. Whether someone is experiencing a mini-transition (or "tune-up" of one's life) or making a life transition into a substantially new direction, coaching may be asked for. As coach, you assess the client's current situation and preferences and then identify specific steps that need to be taken. The vignette provided by Barbara Doyle, about an architect switching careers in his forties, demonstrates how, through coaching, the client was able to clarify his goals, assess his situation, and get the support he needed to take concrete steps in a new direction.

Integrating assessments into transition coaching and the development of strategic life plans often helps clients increase their self-awareness and provides coaches useful data. Your understanding the "entrepreneurial style" of your clients, based on the Myers-Briggs Type Indicator, will help you develop life plans that fit with your clients' dominant approach to living. Another important part of this coaching process is helping your clients clarify their values so that they can arrive at a vision of their ideal life and then craft a plan to make it a reality.

Executive Coaching and Leadership

O ne of the most exciting opportunities in executive coach ing is leadership development. Both individuals and orga- nizations are increasingly turning to coaches to foster the development of leadership competencies, resulting in an increased demand for effective leadership coaching. Beyond the professional opportunities that result, by coaching leaders we can exert a powerful positive influence that touches hundreds and even thousands of oth- ers who are affected by our clients' leadership.

What are the competencies of great leaders? How can coaches help leaders unleash their fullest potential? Warren Bennis, one of the most outstanding researchers and writers on the qualities of effective lead- ership, writes:

> *Leaders are people who are able to express themselves fully ... they know who they are, what their strengths and weaknesses are, and how to fully deploy their strengths and compensate for their weaknesses. They also know what they want, why they want it, and how to communicate what they want to others, in order to gain their cooperation and support. Finally, they know how to achieve their goals.[1]*

What aids executives in expressing themselves fully, thereby pro- viding a pathway that business guru Bennis feels is essential to effec- tive leadership? Bennis responds, "The key to full self-expression is understanding one's self and the world, and the key to understanding is learning—from one's own life and experience." Experienced thera- pists, with their background in helping people examine their cogni- tive processes and communicate their feelings, have the skills to help executives develop this type of learning.

Another angle on coaching and leadership is provided by Stephen Covey, who popularized the value of developing effective internal habits and transferring them into a personal leadership style with his books *The Seven Habits of Highly Effective People* and *Principle-Centered Leadership.* [2,3] The FranklinCovey™ coaching and training organization has reportedly taught his ideas about effective leadership to more than half the Fortune 500 companies.[4] Hence a generation of leaders have at least tangentially been influenced by Covey's concepts of having a personal vision, beginning an activity with your end product in mind, thinking win-win, incorporating empathic communication, developing trust through relationships, creatively cooperating with others, and "sharpening the saw"—that is, engaging in lifelong learning. Executive coaches can be employed to help leaders make these global concepts become personalized, thus increasing their individual effectiveness as leaders. Despite Covey's and other experts' encouragement, however, only a small percentage of executives have actually partnered, one-on-one, with an executive coach to further their leadership development.

Again, professionals with training in psychotherapy are ideally suited to offer this kind of individual coaching. Therapists-turned-coaches can assist clients in deepening their self-understanding and examining their experiences for learning that will aid them professionally and personally.

Of course, coaching for leadership requires relevant study and experience. Ideally, therapists moving into leadership development have experienced leadership roles themselves. In addition, they need to become well versed in the leadership literature and have many in-depth conversations with leaders to deepen their understanding of the challenges of leadership. Moreover, they need to have a thorough knowledge of both the competencies that enable leaders to excel and ways to shape these leadership competencies.

OVERVIEW OF EFFECTIVE LEADERSHIP

Do you have a mental picture of what effective leadership is and of how effective leaders develop? Effective leadership includes mastering a wide range of skills, from introducing and implementing new processes to inspiring excellence in others. Basic leadership competencies include communications skills, coaching others, utilizing authority, delegating, developing others, and facilitating effective teamwork.

From his in-depth study of CEOs, William Bennis concluded that leaders are made, not born. He also found that leaders start out with the motivation to be fully heard and expressed, more than a specific intention to be a leader. He found that the motivation to "be fully heard and expressed" is fundamental to "leading," as opposed to being "driven."[5]

Becoming a leader is similar to becoming an integrated person in the sense that a well-balanced character is central to effective leadership. Leaders of effective organizations create a culture of respect, trust, and caring by communicating to others clear goals, vision, conviction, and passion. Finally, Bennis asserts, "Generating and sustaining trust is the central ingredient in leadership."[6]

James Kouzes and Barry Posner, like Bennis, conducted an in-depth study of outstanding leadership.[7] They collected hundreds of case studies of leadership from people in many different types of organizations and from leaders at lower management levels to the most senior executives. Here are Kouzes and Posner's five leadership dimensions, their corresponding connections to Bennis and Nanus's management research, and based on these characteristics, some of my favorite coaching inquiries to foster effective leadership:[8]

1. Challenging the process: They found that effective leaders searched for opportunities, experimented and took reasonable risks to help their organization. Bennis and Nanus referred to this as "management of risk."

- What do you find as fun or exciting about trying something new?

- What is a way you can take initiative to overcome an obstacle?

2. Inspiring a shared vision: Leaders see their vision, then they learn how to communicate their vision in a manner that taps the dreams of their constituents. This is similar to what Bennis and Nanus called the "management of communication."

- What do you find most inspiring?

- What are some ways you can effectively share your vision with others?

3. Enabling others to act: Kouzes and Posner contend that leaders foster a team effort by promoting collaboration through relationships and supporting personal development. These behaviors are similar to what Bennis and Nanus call "management of risk."

- Describe a situation when you felt empowered by what a leader told you. How did you feel and what did you do?

- What kind of training or support can be provided to help specific team members move forward?

4. Modeling the way: Leaders model the way through their personal example and their observable dedication. This is what Bennis and Nanus call "management of trust."

- What do you need to start doing to "model the way"?

- In what ways can you support and highlight your employees values that are congruent with the principles that you are promoting?

5. Encouraging the heart: Great leaders notice and celebrate their follower's contributions and achievement. Encouraging the heart parallels what Bennis and Nanus call "management of respect."

- ■ In what way can you increase your personal recognition and public praise of individual employees?

- ■ What inspiring story can you tell others this week that highlights the contribution of one of your team members?

As we proceed through this chapter, we will examine a number of specific areas of leadership competency that lend themselves to coaching.

WHAT IS LEADERSHIP DEVELOPMENT?

Leadership development is important work: the success of a business and the success of society depends on the quality of its leaders. A poor leader can quickly take a great company, or even an entire country, to ruin. Conversely, great leaders can create not only business success but opportunities for personal fulfillment for many people.

Patagonia: A Deep-Seated Commitment to Environmentalism

Spotlight on Yvon Chouinard, Founder and Owner of Patagonia, Inc. the outdoor apparel company based in Ventura, California.

At Patagonia, Inc., a $223 million designer and distributor of rugged, good-looking adventure clothes and equipment, headquartered in Ventura, California, success means much more than just designing and selling the highest quality outerwear. It means making a deep commitment to pressing environmental

...continued on next page

---

and social concerns as well. By developing a socially conscious corporate culture and supporting the environmental causes and groups its customers care most about, Patagonia has hit upon a winning business formula that sets it apart from all other outerwear marketers, and stands as a shining example for all businesses.

Patagonia's founder, and the visionary behind the social responsibility of the company, is Yvon Chouinard. Chouinard has a "doing well by doing good" strategy, which is paying off in outstanding sales and fiercely loyal customers. Chouinard started Patagonia in the late 1960s as a sister to the Chouinard Equipment Company, makers of hardware for alpine climbing. When Chouinard realized that climbing equipment harmed the pristine wilderness setting in which it was used, he decided to make an innovative alternative to the mountain climbing bolts, which were traditionally left in the face of the rock after they were used.

The original Chouinard Equipment Company was sold, but the environmentally responsible tradition goes on at Patagonia. Patagonia takes social responsibility seriously in all aspects of its business, from the materials in its clothing to the construction details in its retail stores, to donating millions of dollars a year to environmental causes.

Chouinard comments, "Perhaps the real good Patagonia could do was by using the company as a tool for social change— as a model to show other companies that you can do well by taking the long view and doing the right thing."

The Center for Creative Leadership, founded in 1970, is one of the world's leading organizations involved in the research of effective leadership development.[9] The Center's research indicates that developing leadership potential requires an ongoing process to expand such capacities as self-awareness, flexibility, initiative, teambuilding, and creativity. Leadership development is never complete; it is an ongoing process. New situations and new challenges continually present new learning experiences, and it is these real-life experiences where the "teeth" of leadership are cut.

What does the process of leadership development look like?

Step 1: Evaluation

The first step is an honest *evaluation* of your client's current leadership abilities and functioning. Formal assessments such as multi-rater feedback tools are helpful, as are honest self-reflection and open conversation between the client and coach regarding how the client handles various situations. An assessment process helps to illuminate gaps between the client's current leadership competencies and the emerging leadership goals. Increasing leadership capacity requires that individuals become open to examining their mental models and their behavior.

As a coach involved in leadership development, much of the core of your coaching will involve the conversations you engage in to help executives clarify their aspirations, facilitate their abilities, and produce desired results. As part of your assessment and rapport building process with your executive clients, you can adapt the questions that Warren Bennis and his colleague Burt Nanus asked in their groundbreaking research, which involved sixty in-depth interviews with CEOs. The understanding you gain can help you to design a coaching agenda that takes into account the strengths your clients bring to their leadership roles out of their experiences and beliefs.

The questions that Bennis and Nanus posed are:

- What do you believe are the qualities of leadership?

- What do you believe are the qualities of being an effective executive in your field?

- Would you tell me about some of the most important experiences that you had that shaped your development?

- What were the turning points in your life?

- What role has failure played in your life?

- Are there people in your life, or in general, whom you particularly admire?

- What can organizations do to encourage or stifle leaders?[10]

When one of my clients relates a story about a particular leadership challenge or failure, two of my favorite questions to pose are "As you recount this experience, think about what learning—that you especially appreciate—is occurring." and "How can this learning be of assistance to you now?"

Step 2: Challenge

The second step in leadership development is *challenge*. Reflect on your own life for a moment. When did you grow and develop the most? Was it when things were going easily or was it when you were in a challenging situation that pushed you to stretch your capabilities and performance? As your own experience probably attests, sufficient challenge is necessary to move people out of their comfort zones so they will develop new skills or improve their current skills. Without sufficient challenge the motivation to push oneself is low.

What situations are challenging? Novel situations inherently contain an element of challenge. Stretch goals are by nature challenging goals. Managing conflict and managing complexity are challenging. Furthermore, dealing with disappointment, losses, or failures is usually challenging. These situations provide both the opportunity and the motivation for development.

Optimal development occurs when situations contain an appropriate level of challenge. Too little challenge will not be motivating, while too much challenge can be overwhelming and cause poor performance. Coaches help with the challenge step by facilitating clients to take on a realistic challenge, one that fits with their most important values and will lead them to the desired development. Moreover, coaches facilitate challenge in the areas of developmental needs as indicated by the assessment process.

Step 3: Support

The third step in leadership development is *support*. Providing support is one of the key roles that coaches can play as leaders strive to develop their leadership competencies. Support encourages continued engagement through challenging situations. Support provides a reinforcing structure for taking on the challenge and doing the hard work required to meet it. Support also provides an emotional buttress that allows people to go farther than they could go without it.

FOSTERING LEADERSHIP COMPETENCY THROUGH COACHING

Leadership, by its nature, is multidimensional, and as I noted earlier, the process of leadership development never ends. Thus, coaches can intervene in different areas of leadership and work with individuals at different levels depending on the client's existing competencies and stage of development as a leader. Next we will investigate some of the main areas in which coaches may work with clients to improve their leadership.

Core Leadership Competencies

Among other important elements, some of the most important competencies of executive leadership are the abilities to integrate data, communicate meaningfully, and build relationships. In this sense, leadership is a psychological process that takes place in a psychological environment. Of course, leadership involves a high degree of competence in relating to others. Leaders who are adept at flexing their style to maximize the potential of their team members have a competitive advantage. Roger Pearman writes, "Leadership is the process used by anyone, regardless of rank, to create a meaningful collaboration among individuals for a common purpose."[11]

Roger Pearman describes six mental challenges that must be handled well to be a competent leader:

- Communication

- Problem management

- Learning and development

- Blindspots

- Team building

- Values and culture[12]

As a coach you can help executives *identify their communication habits* and acknowledge their behaviors. Coaching can help individuals understand differences in communication styles and improve the communication process with similar and different types of personalities. Improved communication fosters greater understanding and smoother working relationships.

During the coaching process you can help executives recognize the following different stages that they engage in while *problem solving.* Coaches can help clients problem solve by helping them to identify facts, listen for differences in perspective or understanding, clarify distortions, consider effects of decisions on their system, and manage the solution process over time while being aware of any unintended consequences.

Coaches promote the value of *lifelong learning and the development of leadership skills* as central to individual and organizational success. Coaching helps clients clarify their potential areas of learning and develop specific plans to address these areas, taking into account a client's strengths and preferences. Sometimes your clients are best served by your ability to aid them in examining their specific mental processes and experimenting with new behaviors.

A coach is a valuable ally for the executive in helping illuminate *blindspots* through feedback processes and tools. Blindspots are ways in which individuals affect others unknowingly, without awareness of those outcomes. After helping clients see and understand their blindspots, you can encourage them to recognize their own habits and styles. If appropriate, you aid your clients in observing any unintended consequences they are triggering, and you assist them in making behavioral changes. You can then assist them to develop a tailored, focused development plan to support those intended changes. You support the clients' development by helping them craft exercises or homework to experiment with modifying a behavior and by validating their learning and new habits.

Coaches can also work with clients on issues of *team building, organizational values* and *creating a learning organization.* I discuss these aspects of leadership coaching later in this section.

Developing Leadership Competencies Related to Higher Salary

Another viewpoint on leadership competencies is provided by research by David McClelland and Hay/McBer concerning executives at PepsiCo, which found that high development in eleven specific leadership competencies was linked to higher performance-based salary bonuses.[13] As a coach involved in the business and art of leadership development, you can facilitate your clients' development in each of these eleven areas:

1. Self-confidence: Engages in independent action and decision-making, projects professional presence, and embraces challenge.

2. Adaptability: Flexibly adapts to emerging situations,

continues to think despite ambiguities, and adapts strategically as appropriate.

3. Achievement orientation: Creates challenging goals, incorporates cost-benefit analyses into decision making, plans to navigate obstacles, and takes risks after thoughtful analysis.

4. Initiative: Tackles current and future opportunities; is inventive and fast; starts activities early that would have become urgent later.

5. Organizational awareness: Takes into account the organizational culture, informal alliances, internal politics, and the big-picture issues when taking actions.

6. Empathy: Practices inquiry as part of communication style, incorporates active listening, notices nonverbal cues, values diversity, and strives to understand and learn from other perspectives.

7. Developing others: Communicates faith in other people's abilities; provides genuine, consistent feedback; spends time getting to know and supporting others.

8. Communication: Develops a personally engaging style, communicates messages and expectations clearly, listens to other perspectives and concerns before trying to advocate his or her own position, and tailors communication to the audience.

9. Teambuilding: Communicates optimistic expectations, facilitates input, expresses value for diversity, supports team members, and engages in activities that build team spirit.

10. Influence: Cultivates respect, is fluid with specific facts, anticipates reactions of others, is flexible and inventive in utilizing indirect influence and piecing together complex influence strategies to affect outcomes.

11. Leadership: Utilizes a combination of formal and informal authority, personally expresses optimism, has a compelling vision, and fosters commitment and enthusiasm while adapting his or her style to the developmental level of followers.

Leadership Style

Leadership coaching frequently involves helping a leader, often an already exceptional individual, develop or refine his or her leadership style. The executive coach will often be engaged in conversations with clients about what leadership styles are appropriate for their situations. Effective leaders need to consciously choose when, and in what combination, to

- promote an ethic of questioning
- engage in a leadership development role
- adopt a coaching and teaching role
- utilize a forceful execution role
- foster a collaborative process
- take a hands-off approach
- focus on a supportive, encouraging role[14]

Leadership style is the focus of the management ideas popularized by Kenneth Blanchard, Paul Hersey, and colleagues, particularly in their One Minute Manager® series.[15, 16, 17, 18] Blanchard identifies four leadership styles that fit with four development levels of employees. Executive coaches working in a leadership development role should become familiar with this basic leadership philosophy, which is often taught in business school. Briefly, Blanchard recommends the following:

1. Use a *directive style* with an employee who is high in commitment and low in competence. A directive style includes giving specific directions and closely monitoring performance on the job task.

2. Use a *coaching style* with an employee who is low in commitment and relatively low in competence. In this context, a "coaching style" refers to giving specific directions together with an explanation of those directions, solicitation of the employee's own ideas, and a supportive relationship.

3. Use a *supporting style* with an employee who has variable commitment and moderate to high competence. A supporting style provides less specific direction, but facilitates and supports the employee's efforts and invites the employee to share in the decision-making process.

4. Use a *delegating style* with an employee who is high in commitment and high in competence. A delegating style means turning over the responsibility for problem solving and decision making to a highly competent and internally motivated employee with very little specific direction and less frequent need for support.

Coaches will want to adapt this leadership philosophy to the particular situations of their clients, including the developmental level of the leader, as well as the employees they are leading. Thus, as a coach you would counsel varying adjustments in style according to the client's circumstances. For example, when coaching a manager who has just created a new team and finds the employees are predominantly of high competence and variable commitment, you would coach your client in using a supportive role of praising, facilitating, and listening rather than a highly directive, command-and-control style. In this example the high competence level of the employees suggests that a highly directive style would be unnecessary. Such a style would be unattractive to the employees and probably resented by them, as well as a poor use of the manager's time. On the other hand, a manager who leads a group of eager but not yet competent trainees might be coached to modify her usual facilitative style in favor of a more directive style that better meets the needs of the situation.

The Case of Peggy Dynamo

Edward H. Rockey, Ph.D., MPEC

Peggy Dynamo, head of a project team for a major biotech company, was very aware of one career reality and quite oblivious to another. On the one hand, she knew she was a powerhouse leader and that she enjoyed fulfilling such traditional leadership roles as directing, organizing, and controlling. On any inventory that measures things like "Assertive-Directive" or "Need for Power" she would score high on the tendency to take charge. She knew this. Interestingly,, her style in going about taking over did not come across as obnoxious, threatening, or sinister. She was just a straightforward, no-nonsense, bright, take-charge person. A bit brisk, perhaps, but not power hungry or dictatorial.

What Peggy seemed unaware of pertains to two key leadership issues. (1) Peggy was insufficiently attentive to the idea that "people support what they help create." When employees contribute to a plan or solution, they are more likely to experience ownership and commitment. (2) Peggy was also tuning out her failure to help her employees grow to their full potential. Call it empowerment, call it delegation, call it participation, call it employee development, it's a vital part of effective leadership. The best managers have as part of their personal philosophy, "My executive responsibility includes guiding my staff toward the best performance and highest personal development of which they are capable." Of course, this also fits in well with the succession policy that many highly successful organizations follow: every leader must identify one individual who is ready, willing,

...continued on next page

and able to succeed the leader. Such inevitabilities as resignations, promotions, transfers, and deaths make such a policy essential—to say nothing of giving hope to ambitious subordinates.

In a typical meeting, whenever an issue came up for consideration, team deliberation pretty much stopped cold whenever Peggy made a suggestion. Granted, her ideas were almost always sound; she was likely to come up with workable, feasible, well-grounded solutions. But this left some project team members uninvolved and underdeveloped.

Ms. Dynamo's learning style or decision-making style also played a part. Such mottos as "Get it done now" and "Try something; don't just sit on your hands" were both part of her outlook on life. What was hazardous here was the likelihood that other styles were probably needed to complement hers. The deliberate planner, the creative brainstormer, and the careful check-upper are required to effectively round out any significant decision, especially if the plan about to be implemented is an intuitive, quick, "seat-of-the-pants" idea.

Recently Peggy told me that in a vital decision-making meeting she recalled a coaching session we had on her leadership style, and she paused to say to herself, "Aha! Bulldozing again! Take a breath." Federal regulatory agency rules and standards must be scrupulously followed in her company. The meeting agenda included a discussion of how to be sure that mandates were being followed. Peggy was about to push her solution, but she noticed that one quiet, reserved, able employee was taking a back seat in the meeting. Instead of plopping out her solution, Peggy took the time to ask him directly what he had to suggest, and this allowed him to make a valuable contribution.

It's not likely that a leader will change his or her basic nature. Peggy will probably always be more assertive than most. But effective coaching makes us aware that we can change our behaviors. In Peggy's case, it's gratifying to note that Ms. Dynamo is still dynamic but that she is also more likely to develop others and to include their valuable input. Also, happy to relate, she recently received a promotion to greater leadership responsibilities at her biotech company.

Leading Effective Teams

Another way that you can be of assistance to leaders is in helping them develop well-functioning teams. In this role, you support and coach leaders as they strive to bring out the best in their team members, for example, by creating an effective interchange of ideas on the team and by valuing the diversity and uniqueness of team members. You can assist in fostering effective, productive, synergistic relationships with the team members by supporting the leader in promoting a climate of valued interchange.

You may also find yourself called upon to help leaders foster improved performance in an organization through a deliberate focusing on core values. Values are elevated in organizations when the leaders help foster respect for the variety of values present. As a coach, you can emphasize the ways in which respect for diverse values can further organizational success. So, for example, you may facilitate an effort by leaders and groups to clarify their values, such as a greater good for all, autonomy, appreciation, fair play, and allegiance to one's heartfelt concerns. And then you might help them devise ways to concretize these values into action steps.

Building Higher Functioning Organizations

Often a core role of an executive coach is to help facilitate efforts to create a higher functioning organization. You can help organizations improve their functioning by incorporating into your coaching strategy the comments of Harvard's Rosabeth Moss Kanter:

> Adept organizations share three key attributes, each associated with a particular role for leaders:
>
> 1. The imagination to innovate. To encourage innovation, effective leaders help develop new concepts — the ideas, models, and applications of technology that set an organization apart.

2. The professionalism to perform. Leaders provide personal and organizational competence, supported by workforce training and development, to execute flawlessly and deliver value to ever more demanding customers.

3. The openness to collaborate. Leaders make connections with partners who can extend the organization's reach, enhance its offerings, or energize its practices.[18]

Building on Moss Kanter's ideas to improve performance, one way to help the executives in organizations you work with is to create discussions around questions such as "In what ways are you working with your team to enable your organization to be flexible in terms of new opportunities?", "In what specific ways does your organization ensure that it is does everything possible in order to retain your best employees?" and "What are some of the rewards you give your employees who innovate?"

Leading a Learning Organization

Finally, an executive coach may be able to help leaders create a learning organization, as described by Peter Senge. Senge's book, *The Fifth Discipline: The Art and Practice of the Learning Organization,* has sold over 400,000 copies and has created awareness of systems processes in organizations among tens of thousands of managers. Therapists are likely to appreciate and quickly grasp this system orientation because of the overlap with systems training that most therapists receive in graduate school. As Director of the Center for Organizational Learning at MIT's Sloan School of Management, Senge has promoted the concepts that vision, values, integrity, dialogue, and systems thinking are necessary to help organizations learn quickly in order to adapt fast enough to remain successful. Senge's central concept is that organizations perform *because of how we think and how we interact. Only by changing how we think can we change deeply embedded policies and practices. Only by changing how we interact can shared visions, shared understandings, and new capacities for coordinated action be established ... It is challenging to think that while we redesign the manifest structures of our organizations, we must also redesign the internal structures of our mental models. But anything less will fall short of the changes required."[19]*

According to Senge, learning organizations are characterized by the ability to have the entire organization involved in open dialogue, examining interactions systemically. Leaders have a fundamental role in establishing the value of a learning organization and nurturing its culture. In turn, coaches can help nurture a community of learners among the people they work with. As coaches, we can inspire and guide our clients to integrate their vision, values, purpose, systems thinking, and mental models. Then our clients can help create organizations that can learn and adapt in a creative, powerful manner while striving to keep the momentum of the organization on track with its values and core business purpose. Further, through our one-on-one efforts with our clients, leaders are helped to develop their own personal mastery, and the confidence and clarity of thinking to share their own personal vision. A powerful coaching goal is to help our clients develop greater effectiveness in communicating their commitment to their organization's purpose and then aiding them in adopting a style of drawing out of their followers their own way of fitting congruently with the organization's goals. In this way we help leaders unleash the creative potential and the drive of their followers.

SUMMARY

Facilitating the development of leaders is one of the principal roles of executive coaches. Although psychotherapists can call upon their prior training and experience to fill this role, they also need to become familiar with the literature on both leadership and management. In addition, in order to further develop their understanding, they need to have in-depth conversations with leaders. These steps require drive, intellectual horsepower, and self-confidence in the therapist-turned coach.

Leadership development consists of three steps: evaluation, challenge, and support. There are many areas in which coaches can help clients enhance their leadership skills, including expanded problem solving, adapting their communication style to their followers' preferences, overall leadership style, effective team building, and the facilitation of a learning organization. In the next chapter, we turn to another area in which executive (and personal) coaches can be of great assistance to leaders and other clients—emotional intelligence.

CHAPTER	**Emotional**
10	**Intelligence and**
	Coaching

We all know individuals with high IQ who have failed miserably at life. IQ, or cognitive intelligence, predicts school performance well, but not life and career performance. Alternately, Daniel Goleman's popular books, *Emotional Intelligence*[1] and *Working with Emotional Intelligence*[2], have popularized how central emotional intelligence is to career success. Goleman has developed into a respected guru for the business community by appearing regularly in the prestigious *Harvard Business Review* touting the benefits of increased emotional intelligence—including higher executive salary. Furthermore, Goleman stresses that a key method to increase emotional intelligence is through coaching.

Here are two examples from my own experience and practice that illuminate how different levels of emotional intelligence can have an impact on people and organizations.

The Case of Dr. R.

Dr. R. was Chief of Psychiatry at a large medical center that was going through a hostile takeover. As part of the political shenanigans that occurred, Dr. R. published a prominent editorial in the local newspaper proclaiming that the behavioral health department was in a crisis, that some patients were being treated by social workers and other mental health professionals without ever seeing a psychiatrist, and that as a consequence patients were at risk of dying. As you can imagine, the fine psychologists, social workers, and marriage and family therapists in the department were incensed. Employees' motivation to stay with an organization where they were already overworked waned even further now that one of the new leaders was so callously offensive to their professionalism. The employees' anger and frustration interfered with their productivity as they worried that their jobs might not be secure since this leader did not seem to value them.

At the time, I was chief of the psychology department. At a high-level meeting with the hospital administrators, Dr. R., and the other department chiefs, I tactfully, but clearly, condemned the publication of such a letter, challenging how such a public criticism would be helpful to the change process, morale, or public confidence in the health care system. Several of the other chiefs voiced their concurrence.

You can imagine my shock when immediately after the meeting, Dr. R. rushed up to me and said, "Dr. Auerbach, I'm so glad to get to speak with you. I was hoping that you would join me in co-authoring my next editorial for the newspapers." I was stunned. I replied, "Dr. R., I just got done publicly stating my opposition to writing a public letter and my urging of working out differences out of the public spotlight." Needless to say, Dr. R. seemed completely oblivious to my concerns, his colleagues' concerns, and the impact he was having on the organization!

The Case of Jack the Printer

Jack P. had been raised in the family printing business. When he was forty, his father turned over the business to him. The company continued to grow steadily, and after five years Jack took his biggest step—acquiring a printing house in a neighboring city.

Jack's company had twenty-five employees, and the company he purchased had twenty. Jealousy, fear, competition, and power struggles quickly appeared among the employees after the merger. Instead of ignoring the problem or letting it blow up, Jack chose to intervene.

First he noticed how the changes and gossip made him tense and worried. However, he maintained control of his words and behaviors, carefully observing and listening to others empathetically. Jack made a point to speak with all the employees privately about their concerns. He took responsibility to help improve morale, conveyed his vision of keeping all current customers and current employees through the transition, and communicated courage and personal resolve.

Can you guess the sequels to the stories I just related? In the case of Dr. R., the mental health professionals at the medical center continued to feel unappreciated, criticized, and undervalued. In part because of the attitudes conveyed by Dr. R.'s letter, in a two-year period over a third of the staff resigned—more than two hundred professionals! In contrast, Jack's employees felt inspired and admired his leadership. Jack succeeded in retaining all his clients and employees, and his company continued his healthy growth rate.

Both Dr. R. and Jack had major impacts on their organizations. We could say that Jack handled his situation far more capably and intelligently than Dr. R., but what distinguishes the two men is not intelligence in the usual sense, that is, as measured by IQ. If anything, Dr. R., a highly educated professional, had more obvious credentials in this regard. Instead, Jack's superior competency is better described in terms of emotional intelligence.

As these two stories suggest, emotional intelligence is powerfully related to professional and career success. For this reason, it is often a productive focus in coaching.

This chapter explores how coaches can work with individuals and organizations to enhance emotional intelligence. To begin, let's take a more formal look at the concept of emotional intelligence.

WHAT IS EMOTIONAL INTELLIGENCE?

Howard Gardner proposed the idea of "multiple intelligences" in 1983. Gardner's construct included the concept of "knowing one's inner world and being socially adept."[3] This concept of multiple types of intelligence set the stage for the study of emotional intelligence.

Definitions of Emotional Intelligence

Different researchers have defined emotional intelligence differently. Three of the most prolific researchers and teams in the emotional intelligence field are Daniel Goleman and Richard Boyatzis, John Mayer and Peter Salovey, and Reuven Bar-On. To make matters complicated, they all have different definitions of emotional intelligence.

Richard Boyatzis, Daniel Goleman, and Kenneth Rhee have stated that "emotional intelligence is observed when a person demonstrates the competencies that constitute self-awareness, self-management, social awareness, and social skills at appropriate times and ways in sufficient frequency to be effective in the situation."[4] Reuven Bar-On prefers to use the term "noncognitive intelligence." Reuven Bar-On coined the term "EQ," for Emotional Quotient, in 1985 to denote a measure of this type of intelligence. He defines noncognitive intelligence as "an array of emotional, personal, and social abilities and skills that influence one's ability to succeed in coping with environmental demands and pressures."[5]

In 1990, psychologists Peter Salovey, from Yale, and John Mayer, currently from the University of New Hampshire, published a comprehensive theory of emotional intelligence. Mayer and Salovey described emotional intelligence as the ability to identify and monitor one's own feelings, accurately perceive others' feelings, and utilize feelings to guide thought and action. Since then they have published extensively in the emotional intelligence field.[6]

Although there are differences in the formal definitions of emotional intelligence, my colleagues and I have found that clients eagerly receive the basic concept of emotional intelligence and that integrating this area into coaching is beneficial to them. Clients quickly grasp that by increasing their self-awareness, social awareness, self-management, and social skills they improve their capacity to interact effectively with others, thus enhancing their career and personal success.

Characteristics of High Emotional Competency

Leaving aside issues of precise definition, a useful way to conceptualize emotional intelligence is in terms of a general ability or competency made up of several basic characteristics or skill sets. From this perspective, people who are high in emotional intelligence are skilled in these five areas:

1. Self-awareness: They know what they are feeling, they take those feelings into account in decision making, they have confidence, and they can make a realistic assessment of their own abilities.

2. Self-regulation: They manage their emotions, think before they act, delay gratification to achieve goals, and have the elasticity to bounce back from emotional upsets.

3. Motivation: They are persistent and passionate about their projects for intrinsic reasons, and they energetically pursue their goals.

4. Empathy: They can sense what other people are feeling, are able to develop rapport with different types of individuals, and can adapt their communication to fit with the emotional reactions of other people.

5. Social skills: They utilize their ability to manage emotions and accurately interpret social relationships and interactions to find common ground, build rapport, lead, negotiate, and promote cooperation.

According to Goleman, emotional intelligence tends to increase with age and maturity. Importantly, it can also be learned. The best learning programs to enhance emotional intelligence are individualized programs conducted over time with a coach who has graduate training in psychology and who has undergone specific training in coaching skills.

Utilizing the Boyatzis and Goleman model of emotional intelligence requires a more precise understanding of the idea of "competencies." A competency is a measurable characteristic of a person that differentiates level of performance in a particular job, role, organization, or culture. A competency includes skill and knowledge, but it may also incorporate values, roles, self-image, traits, and motives. For example, if someone has the competency of self-awareness, they will be conscious of their own feelings, they will understand why their various feelings occur, and they can anticipate the implications of their emotions.

Using this definition of competency, we can analyze emotional intelligence or competency into a number of component competencies. Boyatzis and Goleman's current model of emotional intelligence rests on twenty observable competencies clustered into four categories, as shown in Table 1: self-awareness, self-management, social awareness, and social skills.

Table 1. Four Clusters of Emotional Intelligence[7]

What makes Self-awareness?

1. Emotional self-awareness
2. Accurate self-assessment
3. Self-confidence

What makes Self-Management?

1. Self-control
2. Trustworthiness
3. Conscientiousness
4. Adaptability
5. Achievement orientation
6. Initiative

What makes Social Awareness?

1. Empathy
2. Organizational awareness
3. Service orientation

What makes Social Skills?

1. Leadership
2. Communication
3. Influence
4. Change catalyst
5. Conflict management
6. Building bonds
7. Teamwork and collaboration
8. Developing others

The competency of self-awareness is critical to the competencies associated with the self-management cluster. If individuals lack high self-awareness, 96 percent of the time they will not demonstrate self-management competencies such as self-control, trustworthiness, conscientiousness, adaptability, achievement orientation, and initiative. However, those with sufficient self-awareness have a 50 percent chance of demonstrating the self-management competencies.[8]

Benefits of High Emotional Competency

As I noted at the start of the chapter, we all know people with high IQs who perform poorly in their lives and careers. Research backs up the everyday observation that emotional or social competency is actually a far better predictor than IQ of success on the job and in life generally.

For example, an interesting study conducted by Karen Arnold and Terry Denny at Boston University on valedictorians clarifies that achieving the highest grades in school does not relate to later success. Eighty-one valedictorians in Illinois high schools (those with the absolute highest grades) were followed for ten years. The researchers found that less than 25 percent of them had gone on to achieve excellent success in their professions.[9] An earlier study tracked the achievement of 95 Harvard graduates into middle age. The Harvard alumni who had the highest college test scores did not achieve significantly higher salary, status, life satisfaction, or happiness with friends, family, or marriage than their peers.[10] These studies support the formidable body of research suggesting that academic achievement, and standard measures of intelligence, are not strongly correlated with outstanding career success. In contrast, the factors that are now referred to alternately as emotional intelligence, emotional competency, or emotional quotient are strongly correlated with personal and career success.

The fundamental elements of emotional intelligence noted earlier—self-awareness, self-regulation, motivation, empathy, and social skills—support a variety of skills that have been found to account for 76 percent of the effectiveness of leading managers.[11] Recently the *Harvard Business Review* and other prestigious publications have run many articles asserting that possessing high emotional intelligence is linked to superior career success, including higher income. The practical value of emotional intelligence competencies appears to be supported by Martin Seligman's research on optimism and positive psychology. For example, Seligman found that highly optimistic salespeople made significantly more sales—from a 20 percent to an 84 percent improvement.[12]

Numerous studies elaborate on how emotional competencies relate to outstanding performance. At PepsiCo, a study showed that executives who were high in three sets of emotional competencies were in the top third of their group in terms of salary bonuses awarded for excellent performance. These sets of competencies were (1) adaptability, achievement drive, and initiative; (2) political astuteness, influence and team-building; and (3) self-confidence, developing others, and empathy.[13]

Goleman cites a surprising example of what makes the top 1 percent of computer programmers, those who produce over 1,000 percent more than their peers, so successful. His research concludes that their superior performance is related to behaviors that are linked to emotional intelligence. What are the behavioral competencies of star computer programmers? These exceptional high performers take the time to help other co-workers, to share ideas, and to collaborate. These behaviors relate to the emotional intelligence competencies of empathy, initiative, social skills, and achievement orientation.[14]

HELPING CLIENTS IMPROVE EMOTIONAL COMPETENCY

Emotional competency is a particularly fruitful area for coaching. Coaches can help their clients increase their emotional competency by:

- using valid assessments to facilitate an evaluation of clients' current emotional competency

- developing a coaching plan that includes a focus on increasing a specific emotional competency and using appropriate techniques to work with clients in this area

Assessment

The most cutting-edge coaching interventions involve incorporating emotional intelligence assessment into the coaching process. The ability to identify the specific areas where development is indicated provides the coach with a logical jumping-off point to develop a coaching agenda as well as a highly effective sales tool to support the use of coaching. Four of the most popular emotional intelligence assessments utilized by sophisticated coaches are discussed here.

Emotional Competence Inventory (ECI)

Based on the research of Goleman and Boyatzis, the international consulting company Hay/McBer developed the Emotional Competence Inventory (ECI). The ECI is a multi-rater tool that assesses emotional intelligence. In addition to the coaching client, the ECI is also administered to the client's direct reports, peers, and manager. This process of obtaining multiple sources of information provides a more accurate picture by incorporating how others see the client as well as the client's self-perception. In the case of a client who is low on accurate self-assessment, the multi-rater aspect is critical.

The ECI provides emotional intelligence ratings on the four clusters and twenty competencies listed in Table 1. Utilizing the ECI, the coach can provide focused feedback about individual strengths and areas for improvement. The ECI can also be used to review an entire work group to profile its strengths and development needs, yielding an overall picture of the group's emotional intelligence. This type of profile—a "workforce audit"—can indicate key emotional intelligence gaps that may limit performance.

Administering the ECI requires accreditation by Hay/McBer. Several faculty members of the College of Executive Coaching hold this elite accreditation and may be available to provide the consultation service of administering the ECI by special arrangement.

BarOn Emotional Quotient Inventory (EQ-i)

Israeli psychologist Reuven Bar-On created the BarOn Emotional Quotient Inventory, a 133-item, self-report measure. (A multi-rater version of this assessment is under development.) The assessment yields an "EQ" standard score similar to the scores you are familiar with from the Wechsler Intelligence Scales. The mean score is 100 with a standard deviation of 15. The EQ-i provides a total EQ score and five EQ composite scale scores: intrapersonal, interpersonal, adaptability, stress management, and general mood (see Table 2). Bar-On's model then applies the results of those five composite scores to predictions of positive performance and development suggestions for improving emotional intelligence.

Table 2. Composite Scales and Subscales of the BarOn EQ-i[15]

Intrapersonal Subscales:

1. Emotional self-awareness

2. Assertiveness

3. Self-regard

4. Self-actualization

5. Independence

...continued on next page

Table 2. (cont.)

Interpersonal Subscales:

1. Empathy

2. Social responsibility

3. Interpersonal relationship

Adaptability:

1. Reality testing

2. Flexibility

3. Problem solving

Stress Management:

1. Stress tolerance

2. Impulse control

General Mood:

1. Optimism

2. Happiness

Multifactor Emotional Intelligence (MEIS®)

The Multifactor Emotional Intelligence Scale (MEIS®)[16] is based on the work of Mayer and Salovey.[17] The MEIS is an ability test designed to measure the four branches of the emotional intelligence ability model of Mayer and Salovey (see Table 3).

Table 3. What the MEIS® measures

1. Identifying Emotions: the ability to recognize how you and those around you are feeling.

2. Using Emotions: the ability to generate an emotion, and then reason with this emotion.

...continued on next page

Table 3. (cont.)

3. Understanding Emotions: the ability to understand complex emotions and emotional "chains," and how emotions transition from one stage to another.

4. Managing Emotions: the ability which allows you to manage emotions in your self and in others.

"EQ Map"

The "EQ Map," developed by Robert Cooper, his colleagues, and Essi Systems, has been pilot-tested on several thousand executives from over 100 United States and Canadian organizations. A 21-scale report is generated after completion of the assessment.[18]

Coaching Suggestions and Techniques

Once you have assessed a client's current emotional competencies and determined a specific area to focus on, the next step is to develop a coaching plan for that area. In doing so, you will, of course, use many of the ideas presented in previous chapters. Here are some additional suggestions and techniques for the specific domain of emotional intelligence.

- Aid your client in developing the skill of holding constructive internal dialogues. For example, if your client feels put down or abused by a superior, you can help the client explore what a helpful inner dialogue would be, such as: "What is the challenge right now that is leading to tension? What feelings do I notice? I know I feel angry right now. What would be a constructive behavior right now? I think it's best not to raise my voice at my boss. I'll get a better outcome if I wait until after the meeting and talk to him privately."

- Because impulse control is an important component of emotional intelligence, teach your clients techniques to manage themselves in stressful situations. The following four-step approach stems directly from cognitive therapy, so mental health practitioners will be well skilled in teaching it to coaching clients: (1) Take two slow abdominal breaths. (2) What am I thinking and feeling? (3) What negative thoughts am I having? (4) What would be a way to rephrase any negative thoughts to more helpful thoughts? (Daniel Feldman describes this technique and others in *The Handbook of Emotionally Intelligent Leadership*.)[19]

- Teach your clients a simple two-step self-coaching approach: (1) What is the positive outcome I want? (2) What are one or two practical steps I will take to achieve that outcome?

- Encourage your clients to have an emotionally intelligent role model. Have them identify someone at work whom they admire for their emotional intelligence. Then they can think, "How would my EI mentor respond in this situation?"

- Assist your clients in developing greater self-awareness by encouraging them to ask themselves questions like these: What am I feeling? How am I acting? What sensations am I having? What do I want? What assumptions am I making?

- Help your clients improve the accuracy of their perceptions by uncovering biases. For example, suppose a client anticipates tension at a certain meeting. Before the meeting, have him write a paragraph about how he views the situation. During the meeting, have your client adopt the attitude of trying to understand the other person's concerns and take some notes about what he is learning from the other person. When you meet with your client, ask him to compare his initial thoughts to what he learned from the other person. Ask your client, "What assumptions, biases, or other perspectives did you realize about the person you were communicating with?"

■ Aid your clients in seeing the advantage of adapting their communication style to their audience. For example, when a client is preparing to communicate a message, ask: "What is important to you about what you plan on communicating? What about your message will be important to your audience? What will be the most effective way to communicate your message? What preparation do you need to do to make sure your message has the desired outcome?"

■ Some of your clients will be in a direct service or sales type of career role where service orientation is closely linked to their income. You can coach clients in understanding how to increase the emotional competency of service orientation by helping them understand their customers' needs from the customers' perspective and to cultivate a clear orientation to meeting their customers' needs. Coach your clients in how to be proactive rather that reactive with their customers. Aid your clients to experience how they can become valued advisors by taking personal responsibility for making sure their customers obtain what they need.

■ To help your clients to increase their competency in managing conflicts, encourage them to bring disagreements into the open. Coach them in how to effectively be aware of and express other people's points of view. Help them see the benefits of focusing on issues, not people, as a method to de-escalate disagreements. Aid your clients in learning to work with people to find win-win solutions when possible.

- Daniel Feldman describes a useful, easy-to-remember technique to help clients operate with high emotional competencies: PRC. (1) *Pause* before you react to a situation. (2) *Reflect* on what is behind any emotions or reactions you are experiencing. (3) *Choose* the appropriate thoughts and actions that will make the situation turn out well.[20]

- Aid your clients in cultivating realistic optimism. Coach your clients in affirming that their efforts will be successful. For example, you can help a client adopt optimistic self-talk, such as "I can do this presentation. I have a solid series of action steps to enable me to prepare thoroughly. I have the support of my coach and several colleagues. I'm right on track."

Improving Emotional Intelligence in a "Command and Control" Manager

Relly Nadler, Psy.D., MPEC

Client Situation: Steve was a 44-year-old mid-level manager with a high tech company that just moved to cross-functional teams. He was named a team leader of a team of nine individuals. Steve was very bright and quick-witted, and he was perceived as arrogant, cold, unapproachable, and not a team player. He would quickly get defensive and sarcastic with peers and could be condescending with his team and the sales force. Steve's supervisor had heard several complaints about his attitude from both the sales team he interfaced with and from others in the organization. Steve worked in operations for fifteen years prior to coming

...continued on next page

to this job. He described himself as a "command and control" type in this previous role. There the typical environment was one of people getting easily irritated and screaming at each other. In this new company the environment was warm and collegial. This was one reason Steve came to the company.

In a joint meeting with Steve and his supervisor that I facilitated, his supervisor shared his concerns about Steve's performance. The following goals were established for him to focus on in his coaching.

1. Be a better listener.

2. Be more responsive to others, such as his team and the sales force, when they made requests.

3. Improve his relationship with the engineering department.

4. Increase his awareness and management of his perceived arrogance with others.

Later Steve added a fifth goal, better awareness and management of his anger and automatic reactive patterns.

Coaching Philosophy: My coaching philosophy is very solution-focused. This is from training as a psychologist in brief therapy, solution-focused therapy, and narrative therapy. I look for strengths to bring into the problem areas. Steve's strengths included being very smart, being a good learner, liking people, and having a positive attitude. Disequilibrium and creative tension were created by who he wanted to be and the contrary feedback he was getting at work. I worked as a "thinking partner" with him to address this gap by providing awareness, clarity, tools, and motivation to make changes. The coaching lasted for about one year.

...continued on next page

Coaching Approach/Activities: A variety of modalities were used with Steve:

- Individual face-to-face coaching twice a month for one to one and a half hours each at his site

- 360-degree feedback and the Myers-Briggs Type Indicator

- Facilitation of a discussion at one of his team meetings about what was and wasn't working with Steve as the team leader

- Two meetings with Steve and his supervisor

- Homework assignments

Steve appeared colder and more aloof to me and to others than he was in reality. This became more apparent when I spent more time with him. He was an ENFJ on the MBTI. Steve's focus on achieving results, compounded by his quick temper, overshadowed his natural preference to connect and contribute to others. After going through his values clarification and mission statement with him, I remember saying, "How come no one knows these sides of you here?" Steve realized he was leaving out some his best parts at work, which he treasured, as would others.

As in any coaching relationship, many things transpired in our coaching. Here are some of the key interventions that helped lead to positive changes for Steve.

1. Values clarification. A structured exercise to identify Steve's top values revealed that his most important values included ethics and honesty, integrity, trustworthiness, productivity, and balance. He realized that his behavior with others wasn't demonstrating honesty, integrity, or trustworthiness. Steve was reacting to situations rather than being who he wanted to be. This

...continued on next page

conversation led to the creation of his fifth goal, better awareness and management of his anger and automatic reactive patterns.

2. Listening skills. Being very bright, Steve had the tendency to give his opinion on things without first inquiring into others' thoughts. This led to some of the perceptions that he was arrogant. We went over a few communication models that emphasized asking more questions and getting others' input before giving his. He quickly realized how he had been putting others off with this pattern of being the expert. Steve became very good at listening to others and developing their ideas.

3. Self-management. Steve and I spent a lot of time talking about what irritates him and how he responds when irritated. He identified having a low frustration tolerance. His key triggers were made salient, and we discussed different strategies to prevent his irritation along with what to do when he was irritated. Stress management and time management were discussed, and he had homework to try out new behaviors between meetings. Steve got better at managing his emotions, becoming less reactive, and bringing a better perspective to his relationships.

4. Team relations. Steve heard directly from his team via the team meetings and the 360-degree feedback how they perceived him and what he needed to do to make positive changes. He understood what he did that gave the perception of arrogance. Steve became very clear in delegating tasks and how to give them to the right people. He empowered them better by clarifying his expectations. Steve became more accessible and approachable with his team. He also became more explicit in what he was doing in "all those meetings" and how it influenced the company's vision and their direct customers. Steve spent one-on-one time with each of his team members and spent more time with the engineering department. He was able to let out more of his funny and personable nature. We spent time going over his direct reports and strategizing how to better relate to them and develop them using the MBTI as a framework.

COACHING FOR EMOTIONAL INTELLIGENCE IN ORGANIZATIONAL SETTINGS

The Coaching Vignette "Improving Emotional Intelligence in a Command-and-Control Manager" demonstrates clearly many of the methods that a coach would utilize to assist an individual to develop emotional intelligence competencies. Ideally, entire teams or organizations will embark on an emotional intelligence development initiative. A system-wide intervention is especially helpful because if only one individual develops his or her emotional intelligence competencies, other forces operating in the client's system can hinder the long-term retention of the new emotional intelligence behaviors.

Elements of Effective Emotional Intelligence Programs

To assist in the development of effective emotional intelligence development programs suitable for organizations, fourteen elements are presented here.[21]

1. Assess the job: Design training based on a systematic needs assessment.

2. Assess the individual: Tailor training to individual needs.

3. Deliver assessments with care: Use emotional intelligence in delivering initial evaluations of a person's emotional competence.

4. Gauge readiness: Assess for readiness, and if someone is not yet ready, make cultivating readiness an initial focus.

5. Motivate: Make clear how training will pay off on the job or for the individual's career, or be otherwise rewarding.

6. Make change self-directed: Have people choose their own goals for development and help them design heir own plan for pursuing them.

7. Focus on clear, manageable goals: Spell out the specifics of the competency and offer a workable plan to get there.

8. Prevent relapse: Help people use lapses and slip-ups as lessons to prepare themselves better for next time.

9. Give performance feedback: Design into the plan feedback from supervisors, peers, friends—anyone who can help coach, mentor, or give appropriate progress review.

10. Encourage practice: Encourage clients to use naturally arising opportunities for practice at work and at home, and to try the new behaviors repeatedly and consistently over a period of months.

11. Arrange support: Build a network of support and encouragement. Even a single buddy or coach will help.

12. Provide models: Encourage supervisors to value and exhibit the competency; make sure trainers do, too.

13. Encourage and reinforce: Encourage change that fits the values of the organization. Show that the competency matters for job placement, promotion, and performance review. Be sure the organization shows it values the change in a consequential way: praise, a raise, or expanded responsibility.

14. Evaluate: Find measures of the competency or skill as shown on the job, ideally before and after training, and also several months later.

A Model Program: American Express

An interesting model program designed to increase emotional intelligence competencies linked to job performance has been conducted for many years at American Express Financial Advisors. A small group of staff in the life insurance division originally developed the Emotional Competence Training Program in the early 1990s. The program grew out of an effort to discover why more clients who needed life insurance were not buying it. Research suggested that a barrier to making more sales was the financial advisors' emotional reactions to the process. Consequently, the company developed and tested a training program designed to help the advisors cope more effectively with some of the emotional challenges and conflicts that they encountered with their clients. The pilot program developed into the Emotional Competence Training Program.[22]

The program focuses on developing virtually every aspect of emotional intelligence, but especially the competencies of emotional self-awareness, self-control, empathy, communication, and conflict management.

The training program has become a standard part of the training programs for both new advisors and new managers. The sessions for managers are delivered by doctoral-level psychologists, while human resource development staff or experienced senior advisors deliver the rest of the program.

The version of the training program that has been most rigorously evaluated consists of four or five days of training, divided into two segments and separated by one to two months. The first part of the program covers self-awareness and self-management, while the second focuses primarily on interpersonal effectiveness and self-management.

The program begins with a discussion on the nature of emotional intelligence. Next the participants engage in activities to become more aware of what they are feeling at any point in time. Then the participants break into small groups and discuss how emotions affect them in their work. These activities build interest and commitment to the training.

Participants learn how to use self-talk, reframing, and visualization to change their behavior, how to use self-disclosure appropriately to improve relationships with others, how to listen to the feelings and thoughts of others and practice reflective communication, and how to notice and respect interpersonal boundaries and cues that boundaries are being violated. They also learn peak performance and stress management techniques.

Facilitators use a variety of teaching modalities to help the participants learn new ways of thinking and acting, including small group discussions, individual exercises involving drawing as well as writing, demonstrations, clips from popular movies, and participant role plays.

In one study of the effectiveness of the program, 33 advisors completed the Seligman Attributional Styles Questionnaire (SASQ), a measure of optimism and coping skill that has predicted success in life insurance sales in previous research. The results showed that the trained group increased 13.5 percent on the SASQ compared to 0.9 percent for the control group. The trained group also showed a greater increase in total sales revenue—10 percent greater than the control sites and 16 percent greater than the company as a whole. Also, there was an impressive increase in life insurance sales—20 percent more sales than control sites and the company as a whole.

SUMMARY

The ability to help clients increase their emotional intelligence is a valued skill for personal and executive coaches. Research indicates that emotional intelligence correlates more strongly with personal and career success than IQ. For this reason, emotional intelligence can be a productive focus of coaching both with individual clients and with organizations.

Although formal definitions of emotional intelligence vary, its fundamental components are self-awareness, self-regulation, motivation, empathy, and social skills. It is useful in coaching to think in terms of a number of competencies that make up overall emotional intelligence, such as the twenty competencies identified by Boyatzis and Goleman. Coaching can then focus productively on specific competencies.

As with other areas of coaching, coaches can assist clients in the area of emotional competency through accurate assessment and creation of a specific and goal-oriented coaching agenda. A number of techniques are especially useful in this domain of coaching. As an experienced mental health professional, you will find many of these techniques familiar.

In working with organizations, coaches may be involved in developing a program to enhance employees' emotional intelligence. The elements of effective programs discussed in this chapter, along with the example of a model program, illustrate how coaches can have a large impact on the emotional intelligence development of individuals and organizations.

chapter 11

Coaching for Personal and Professional Development

Patrick had a problem. He was competent technically with the details of his job at a fast-growing biotechnology company. He also had great one-on-one relationships with people. He wanted to receive a promotion, and top management viewed him as a possible star. But Patrick had a serious deficiency: he was completely ineffective speaking in front of groups. Whenever he got up to speak at a meeting, which was rare, he seemed to lose all confidence, become very meek, and have trouble getting to the point.

Patrick received feedback from the senior team that he needed to act more decisively and confidently in public presentations if he was to be promoted. Rather than leaving Patrick to wonder how he could gain those qualities, the company brought in a coach to help this young executive develop his decision-making and public speaking skills.

People face an array of developmental needs that, when met, help them to be more effective in their careers and in their personal lives. Coaches often help individuals identify and achieve ways that they can be more effective in their personal lives, and they help managers and executives create development plans to enhance their careers. Coaching for personal or professional development is one of the most highly valued and highly reimbursed coaching roles.

Here are a few common developmental goals your clients may face:

- To act more decisively
- To be less dominating

- To manage time effectively
- To delegate more frequently
- To value diversity
- To create alliances
- To build effective teams
- To smooth "rough edges"
- To be more assertive
- To be more generous
- To think more strategically
- To develop a broader perspective
- To increase confidence
- To become a more effective communicator

Coaching for personal or professional development builds on the principles and skills presented in previous chapters. This chapter discusses some additional considerations you should have in mind when you engage in this kind of coaching.

THREE-ELEMENT DEVELOPMENT COACHING: EVALUATION, CHALLENGE, AND SUPPORT

To help your clients reach developmental goals, you must help them:

1. Evaluate their skills, identify their developmental goals, and create a developmental plan.

2. Seek appropriate challenges.

3. Find adequate support to meet those challenges.

These three elements of evaluation, challenge, and support are the keys to a productive development experience. They consequently provide the basic skeleton for the developmental coaching process.

Evaluating the Client's Current Situation and Creating a Developmental Plan

The evaluation stage consists of assessments and informal gathering of information to enable you and your clients to understand what they are effective at now, what their current strengths are, and what their developmental needs are. The assessment of a client for developmental purposes includes a thorough conversation with the client and in executive coaching may also include feedback from peers, the human resources department, supervisors, or direct reports. Other helpful assessment techniques for the client are personal reflection, responses to journal writing, and other homework assignments. The coach can also ask the client to seek feedback from peers on how he or she handled a particular situation. The information gathered from all these sources can then be incorporated into the development planning process.

Here are some questions you might ask clients in the evaluation and planning stage of developmental work:

- What challenges have you had?
- What lessons have you learned from your challenges?
- What challenges would you benefit from?
- Would you like to take some assessments that I have found helpful for some of my other clients who have been in situations somewhat similar to yours?
- What is your most important developmental need?
- In what situations have you learned the most about yourself?

- In what situations have you felt the most challenged?

- Where and how do you feel the most supported?

In order to craft a developmental plan with the client, schedule a specific coaching session to review the assessments and discuss the steps and resources required to reach the client's developmental goals. Have clients choose the areas they most want to develop—perhaps one to four areas. Discuss these areas in terms of desired outcomes, new skills needed, types of support needed from other people, and a timeline.

Next, work with the client to transfer this discussion into a written development plan. It's a good idea to have a blank development form that your client completes. In order to maintain high internal commitment, have the client take responsibility for creating the development plan as much as possible. Figure 1 shows a sample development plan.

Figure 1. Development Plan Example

Name _____ Start Date _____

Next Review Date _____

Developmental Target: Team Building

Skills Needed	Planned Activities and Frequency
Cooperates with others	Conduct monthly team building activities
Encourages others	Conduct weekly one-on-one meetings with direct reports
Solicits input from others	Obtain feedback from team members weekly
Builds team spirit	Express positive comments to each direct report weekly Adapt communication style for personality type of direct reports in each weekly meeting

Facilitating an Appropriate Level of Challenge

Clients' developmental goals must be sufficiently challenging to ensure that growth and development occur. When challenge is present, people are stretched beyond their current capabilities. Without adequate challenge, there will not be significant progress or satisfaction. However, if the challenge is too great, a client may feel incompetent. The chances of failure are then increased. Consequently, your task as a coach is to help your clients maintain a course between being underchallenged and overchallenged so that they can make maximum progress with manageable anxiety.

In addition to the challenges inherent in reaching ambitious goals, clients may also face new challenges that arise externally. Some of the situations that commonly lead clients to feel challenged are:

- taking a new job
- acquiring new responsibilities
- starting a new project outside their expertise
- leading a new team or committee
- encountering new personalities that are hard for them to work with
- discovering a need to broaden their perspectives

In coaching for development, you will need to be sensitive to circumstances that increase the level of challenge involved in reaching the client's developmental goals. Again, an overabundance of challenge will increase the chances of failure. As the level of challenge increases, clients may need increased levels of support to compensate.

Supporting the Client's Development

An essential element that facilitates development is the support the coach provides. Support increases clients' motivation to continue to put forth their best efforts in the face of difficulties. Clients need to believe that their efforts to reach a particular developmental goal will be successful. The greater their belief, the greater their self-efficacy. In turn, the greater their self-efficacy, the greater their motivation.

Coaches provide a supportive mechanism for making realistic progress by giving effective feedback, helping clients increase their confidence in new situations, and holding clients accountable to their step-by-step action plans. A few more ways that you can provide your client with support follow.

You can ask:

- "In what ways could I be of support for you?"
- "What new skills will you need?"
- "Where and how can you learn those skills?"

You can also:

- Reinforce targeted training.
- Introduce your client to new skills.
- Role-play new skills and behaviors.
- Provide emotional encouragement.
- Aid in developing realistic, doable action steps.
- Help your clients be accountable for their reasonable plans.
- Cheerlead progress.

- Share occasional motivational examples and metaphors.

- Be an ally.

- Provide ongoing feedback.

In addition to the direct support you provide, you can also help clients create the additional supports they need to enhance their self-confidence, utilize their strengths, and manage challenges. As I noted a moment ago, when clients are facing major challenges, they may need additional levels of support to compensate. Some specific ways clients can add more support with your facilitation and encouragement include the following:

- Working directly with you

- Enlisting the aid of significant others

- Obtaining additional help or supportive feedback from co-workers or managers

- Delegating when appropriate

- Getting additional training

- Deepening their spiritual practice

Providing Support Through Effective Feedback

Ana Maria Montes, Ph.D., MPEC

Fred M. is in his early forties and is a manager in a large national organization. His goal is to move up in the organization and head one of the regional offices. Fred wants to develop and polish his leadership skill so that he can reach his goal.

Fred was given a series of assessment tools and had conversations with his boss. I observed him at a meeting of his peers. Afterward, I met with him, reviewed some of the assessment data with him, and incorporated the observations that I had made during the peer meeting. The following conversation illustrates the process of providing support for developmental change through effective feedback.

Coach: Fred, your FIRO-B indicates that you probably have a high need to be accepted and included in the activities of others. People with these scores tend to request approval from others. Earlier we were talking about this, so do you think that these scores reflect you accurately?

Fred: Yes, they do. I can see what you were saying and how sometimes I don't want to confront people and sometimes I wait too long.

Coach: It seems from the other scores in your 360-degree assessment that this high need for approval colors many of your behaviors and decisions.

Fred: My boss told me I was too nice.

Coach: What did he mean by that?

...continued on next page

Fred: I don't know, he did not specify. He could not give me any examples, he said that I was just too nice.

Coach: You know, Fred, when I was observing you the other day with your peers, I noticed that when someone made a comment that appeared critical of another member, you jumped in and made a comment that would justify or somehow soften the comment of the other person. Have you noticed yourself doing what looks like some form of rescuing behavior?

Fred: I had not noticed that.

Coach: For example, when Marlene was giving Adam feedback about how he had come across as very harsh, you made a comment about how Adam had to operate that way, because he was in a managerial role, and that at other times he doesn't talk like that.

Fred: You are right—I did that, I do that. I'm wondering if that is what my boss is talking about.

Coach: Another thing that came out of your scores that also appears to be related is unwillingness to let others make mistakes—how you give responsibilities to them, but then take them back if the job isn't done right.

Fred: I do want things coming out of my department to be right. I do not want my department to be criticized.

Coach: What do you make out of what we have been talking about so far?

...continued on next page

Fred: I need to stop "rescuing" others and help them, not by trying to fix things for them, but by providing them useful, constructive feedback and asking them relevant questions that will facilitate their growth.

Coach: What do you think you need to do around delegating?

Fred: I need to stop taking away the work that I have given them.

Coach: I agree with you, Fred. When you give and take away, it can lead to people feeling incompetent and stupid. There are a couple of good references that I will share with you around delegating. They can help you with looking at what to delegate, when, and to whom. I think you will find them useful.

Fred: Thanks.

Coach: What steps do you need to take in order to change your old behavior?

Fred: For one thing, I am more aware of what I am doing. I will remind myself not to rescue others.

Coach: Do you have someone at work whom you trust that can give you feedback on this?
Fred: Yes, there are a couple of people who would give me feedback if I asked them.

Coach: That sounds good, Fred.

The Developmental Process in Summary

As coaches interested in facilitating clients' efforts to achieve developmental goals, we either help construct developmental situations that incorporate the cardinal elements of evaluation, challenge, and support or we frame the challenging situations that our clients are encountering in those terms. Then we engage in the coaching process to add the necessary elements to foster as ideal a developmental experience as possible. Some of the activities that we might engage in to facilitate the developmental process include implementing a multi-rater feedback process, co-designing with the client a training experience, mentoring the client, co-creating a developmental job assignment, and coaching the client through a stretch goal (see discussion of stretch goals later in this chapter). These and other activities will result in a more successful developmental experience if the essential components of evaluation, challenge, and support are present.

Your clients will reach their developmental goals by integrating the coaching into their approach to their challenges and by practicing the skills and behaviors that they are trying to improve. You help them design action plans to facilitate the necessary practice. Through practice your clients will learn by doing. Because they are learning from their own experience, the learning feels powerful and tends to create a lasting, significant developmental experience.

HELPING CLIENTS LEARN FROM EXPERIENCE

How do we help our clients to learn from their experiences? The mere fact that a client undergoes an important experience ripe with potential learning doesn't mean that learning will occur. T. S. Eliot said not to "have the experience, and miss the meaning." Some studies suggest that less than 20 percent of the population learn rapidly from their experiences. To develop, we need to have both the motivation and the capacity to learn from significant experiences.

Coaches can help clients learn from their experiences by coaching for client self-efficacy, openness to experience, emotional self-awareness, thinking, conscientiousness, and anxiety management, just to name a few. Here are some additional things you can encourage clients to do in order to learn from their experience:

- Search the past for similar or divergent experiences.

- Ask, "What am I learning from this experience?"

- Visualize different outcomes.

- Gain additional relevant information, for example, by conducting Web searches.

- Experiment.

- Take the next step.

- Seek advice or support.

- Ask, "What would a role model learn from this experience?" or "How would a role model handle this situation?"

- Confront fears and continue to be open to learning.

- Walk along the beach or a trail reflecting on their learning.

- Journal about their learning.

- Discuss with a trusted friend or peer their emerging learning.

FACILITATING THE ACHIEVEMENT OF STRETCH GOALS

Many times clients will be attracted to goals that are a huge "stretch" from where they are now. Often they will not have the resources, experience, or knowledge to achieve these goals on their own. A coach can help clients create realistic plans to reach their lofty destination.

As a coach you help your clients stretch their mental models, vision, courage, and sometimes their endurance. You help your clients brainstorm, explore new opportunities, think outside of the box, and challenge themselves in new ways.

Coaches help clients set stretch goals that are congruent with their highest dreams. In this way you are helping people orient themselves toward striving for their best and for the best of those around them.

When John F. Kennedy and Lyndon Johnson brainstormed on a stretch goal for space exploration, they came up with a goal that motivated a whole country to land a person on the moon. This was a bold, unprecedented step that captured the imagination of the world and set up a stretch between current abilities and new knowledge, behavior, and accomplishments.

The practice of helping people create and achieve stretch goals can be facilitated with individuals or groups. Here are four elements of stretch goals and associated coaching questions.

- Hope: Who do I want to be? Who do we want to be?

- Disparity: A stretch goal is an exciting aspiration that almost seems impossible to achieve because of the gap between where we are now and where we want to be. Helping individuals or groups deliberately create a goal, with a gap between where they are now and where they want to be, with a foundation of dreams and values, can create powerful motivation.

- Synergy: Design your coaching to help clients identify their strengths and resources and bring them together with other individuals on their team. A synergistic effect is created when people are brought together to create more than can be done alone.

- Concentration and Support: Peter Drucker says that

the "most important principle of effectiveness is concentration."[1] Focus on measurable objectives that can be accomplished in weeks or months when fostering stretch goals. The high energy, concentration, and single-minded purpose required to achieve a stretch goal usually requires an "end in sight" to help clients balance their aspirations with other interests and responsibilities, such as family commitments. Also, help clients arrange for extra support in needed areas to facilitate their intense focus and movement. Clients may benefit from coaching in how to delegate other responsibilities so they can have more time and mental focus for their stretch goals.

In more general terms, if you don't encourage a client to stretch, the coaching won't feel very powerful or meaningful to the client. You can help your clients to stretch by asking questions such as these:

- "I have a sense you might be able to accomplish more than you are describing."

- "What would it be like if we shoot even higher?"

- "I have a sense that you could become more of a leader in your field. In what ways might you be holding yourself back?"

When you encounter a client to stretch, you may enter areas that might be outside the client's awareness, and the client may become uncomfortable. What relationship must be in place before clients encounter this more challenging side of the coach? A relationship built on trust, empathy, accurate listening, genuine feedback, and relevant questioning contributes to the rapport necessary for the coach to take on the challenging role of facilitating stretch goals. Without this relationship, the client might feel that "you don't understand what I'm going through." As a coach, you can gauge the client's reaction and lighten up if your challenges get uncomfortable for the client. But how do you know how light to be, versus facilitating the stretch? Keep the conversation going, let the client lead, and usually have the client set the agenda. Remember to pose requests or make suggestions relatively infrequently so the client is maintaining high internal commitment to the coaching.

To build energy and motivation for goals, help your clients create a case for action that includes their reasons why the goal is important to them. Sometimes it is highly motivating to ask, "What would the cost be of not taking this action?" Overall, assist your clients to identify what type of learning is required, highlight the value of lifelong learning, and help your clients obtain the support they need to achieve the stretch.

Coaching a New Executive on a Stretch Goal
Jeffrey E. Auerbach, Ph.D., MPEC

Michael, a Stanford MBA graduate, approached me for coaching because he was having trouble landing a good job despite outstanding graduate school performance. Initially coaching focused on job interview performance. I helped him demonstrate increased assertiveness and confidence and to clearly convey to his interviewer the high level of commitment he was prepared to make. After three months Michael was hired into a ten-million dollar technology company with two owners.

Michael quickly found himself in a situation where he recognized it was necessary to achieve a formidable stretch goal. He had been hired into an organization that was facing possible

...continued on next page

bankruptcy. *Michael was suddenly in a position where he was "stretched" into negotiating with executives with some of the largest technology companies and facilitating the development of a new line of data management software. He made a commitment to learn the business as fast as possible. Michael focused on developing the necessary competencies to succeed and was supported in several practical ways through the coaching relationship.*

The coaching involved being a supportive listener to his stressors, helping him focus on what he could do now or could learn to do, facilitating extra support from myself and other professionals with technical expertise, providing lots of recognition of his progress, and providing encouragement that I believed he could grow into whatever challenge was coming. I also provided him extensive feedback and modeling on communication skills. Eventually I helped him to explore possible co-ownership of the company. Ultimately Michael decided to push for co-ownership since he actually saved the business from bankruptcy.

Through this experience Michael moved through four levels of coaching goals:

- Self-awareness of a need for rapid growth.

- Performance improvement to get hired initially.

- Performance breakthrough to meet the demands of turning the business around.

- Transformation into a co-owner of the business and the recognition and self-confidence that he had transformed himself into an expert capable of holding his own with the other international leaders in his business.

A SYSTEMIC APPROACH TO DEVELOPMENT

In organizational settings, development of individuals' competencies is most successful if the system and culture of the organization support development. Human resource professionals are increasingly knowledgeable about the importance of taking the system into account when hiring executive coaches. Russ Moxley and Patricia O'Conner Wilson of the Center for Creative Leadership have documented how Fortune 500 companies are increasingly seeking developmental experiences for their employees that (1) are process oriented versus one-time training, (2) usually involve multiple types of developmental experiences, (3) take into account the complexity of development, and (4) recognize that the organization's culture and business systems are an important component of the employees' developmental success.

Moxley and Wilson offer this example:

Requests that used to sound like this:

"I have this manager who desperately needs development. She has been given feedback that her performance is not up to par, and the turnover in her department is increasing to levels we can no longer tolerate. She needs to get the message—if you know what I mean—pronto! Which program would you suggest to help remedy this situation?"

Now sound like this:

"I'm interested in engaging one of our high-potential managers in a process of development over time—not a single development experience like a training course. In about five years' time, there is a strong possibility that she will be the leading candidate to head up our largest division. We feel the need to craft a long-term strategy for preparing her to make the leadership contributions we know she will someday be capable of making. Where do we begin?"[2]

Coaches from the mental health field generally are trained in system theory. So we can convincingly convey to human resource professionals, and to other executives in the organizations in which we are consulting, the wisdom that outcomes will be enhanced if organizations assume that responsibility for development will be shared by the individual, his or her manager, the team, human resources, and top executives. Furthermore, the business systems of the organization, such as the budgeting process, the reward and recognition system, and the selection system, should complement, and not hinder, the development system. A practical application would be that the developmental process between coach and employee is kept confidential and that the multi-rater feedback used in coaching is not used in performance reviews. These would be systemic confidence-building measures that would increase employees' freedom to be completely candid with their coach.

SUMMARY

The core of facilitating development in your clients is expanding their capacity to be effective in areas that are important to them, whether in their careers or their personal lives. Although the possible areas of development for which people seek coaching are too numerous to list, some of them include acting more decisively, being less dominating, managing time effectively, delegating more, building effective teams, improving communication, valuing diversity, being more assertive, being more generous, and smoothing "rough edges."

The three necessary elements to include in your coaching for development are evaluation, challenge, and support. Evaluation is a multifaceted process that can include information from a number of sources, from formal assessments to peer feedback to coaching conversations with the client. The information that is gathered in the evaluation stage is incorporated into a challenging, written development plan that includes the necessary supportive processes. Throughout the development process, it is crucial that the challenge components and the support components are in balance. If insufficient challenge is present, the development will not be substantial; if too much challenge is present, the client may not succeed. Coaches also facilitate development by helping clients learn from experience and by helping them devise and reach stretch goals. Landing a person on the moon is an example of one of the greatest stretch goals humans have embarked on and accomplished. The world was engaged in the excitement and challenge of accomplishing a grand goal, when at first we weren't sure how it could be done. To facilitate the achievement of stretch goals, help clients tap into their hopes, the realization of the gulf they need to cross, the value of synergistic relationships, and the power of focused concentration.

Facilitating development in organizational settings is best done via a systemic approach that involves the organization's culture, processes, and people. Fortunately, there is a general trend in Fortune 500 companies to recognize that development is a gradual process versus an event that can occur in a single day of training. Human resource professionals, who often contract for external coaches, are increasingly willing to craft long-term development strategies for promising stars. This view that the organization shares great responsibility for development fits well with the systemic view of development that many therapists are familiar with.

We have now reached the end of this exploration of personal and executive coaching, but your own journey is only beginning. I hope that you are excited about the challenging process of moving forward as a personal or executive coach. I wish you great success as you pursue your personal vision of how you will bring your personality, strengths, experience, and wisdom to this vital and immensely rewarding field.

Appendix

I. New Client Questionnaire

Please take a reasonable amount of time (you define that!) to answer the following questions. There are no right or wrong answers. Some of the questions capture information about where you are today. Other questions will make you curious about what you want from coaching, from your career, and from your life in general. Your answers will help us set a strong foundation for the coaching relationship.

Name: _____

Mailing Address: _____

Home Telephone: _____ Work Telephone: _____

Fax Number: _____ E-mail Address: _____

Occupation: _____

1. What do you want to work on in coaching? _____

_____

_____

_____

2. How do you want me to be as your coach? _____

_____

_____

_____

3. What do you want to be certain to obtain from the coaching relationship? _____

_____

_____

_____

4. What two steps could you take immediately that would help you move forward? _____

_____

_____

5. What can I say to you when you are stuck that will help you move forward? _____

_____

_____

6. What changes need to be made within yourself, or your life, to help your coaching be successful? _____

_____

_____

_____

I. New Client Questionnaire page 2

CAREER

1. What do you want from your career? _____
_____
_____
_____
_____

2. What projects are you involved with? _____
_____
_____
_____
_____

3. What are your key career goals? _____
_____
_____
_____
_____

4. What skills or knowledge are you developing? _____
_____
_____
_____
_____

5. How do your career goals support your personal goals? _____
_____
_____
_____
_____

6. What do you want to do to support your career goals? _____
_____
_____
_____
_____

7. What do you need to change to help your career move forward? _____
_____
_____
_____
_____

I. New Client Questionnaire page 3

PERSONAL

1. What special interests do you have? _____
_____
_____
_____
_____

2. What special knowledge do you have? _____
_____
_____
_____
_____

3. What do you believe in strongly? _____
_____
_____
_____

4. What do you do when things get stressful? _____
_____
_____
_____
_____

5. What activities have special meaning for you? _____
_____
_____
_____

6. What vision do you have for your life? _____
_____
_____
_____
_____

7. Tell me about your family and personal life: _____
_____
_____
_____
_____

8. Tell me about significant events in your life: _____
_____
_____

II. Sample Coaching Agreement

Dear Coaching Client,

I coach my clients by utilizing questionnaires, asking questions, listening carefully to what you tell me, jointly developing relevant homework, identifying your resources (experiences and qualities), creating strategies to overcome blocks to success, working toward a high degree of self-care, and identifying your values and vision. A key aspect of the coaching relationship is on developing appropriate action steps to help you move toward your goals and dreams. Although there are no guarantees on the outcomes from coaching, most people report significant progress on their goals.

Coaching is not therapy. Although I am trained in psychotherapy, I do not engage in the practice of psychotherapy with my coaching clients. If issues arise that are best dealt with in a therapeutic context, I will refer you to an appropriately trained licensed therapist. In entering into the coaching relationship, and signing this agreement, you are agreeing that if any mental health difficulties arise during the course of the coaching relationship, you will notify me immediately so I may provide you with appropriate referrals.

We will agree on a standard time for our telephone consultations. Once that time is established, it will be reserved for you. If you need to cancel an appointment, please provide at least 24-hour notice or you will be charged for the appointment. My fees are $ _____ a month for _____ half-hour coaching appointments. However, additional appointments can be scheduled.

The information you share with me will remain strictly confidential unless (1) you give specific permission to release the information or (2) I am required to release the information by law. Exceptions to confidentiality include information about intent to seriously harm an individual, child abuse, and elder abuse. Be aware that privilege may not apply to coaching; in other words, coaching records may be able to be subpoenaed. Some means of communication, such as wireless telephones and e-mail, may not be secure from eavesdropping, so if you agree to their use you are indicating your agreement to utilize a communication medium that may not be confidential.

Each party agrees to indemnify, defend, and hold harmless the other party and its agents, officers, and employees from and against any and all liability expense, including defense costs and legal fees incurred in connection with claims for damages of any nature whatsoever, including but not limited to, bodily injury, death, personal injury, financial or businesses losses, or property damage arising from such party's performance or failure to perform its obligations hereunder.

Coaching usually leads to improvements and positive changes in one's life. We will discuss the pros and cons of coaching together.

I believe that each of my clients is unique, creative, and responsible for moving their own life forward. I look forward to working with you.

Sincerely,

_____
Personal and Executive Coach   Date

I fully understand and agree to the above document.

_____
Coaching Client Signature   Date

Also, Richard R. Kilburg has provided a less legalistic model agreement for coaching services in Kilburg, R. R. (2000). *Executive coaching: Developing managerial wisdom in a world of chaos.* Washington, D.C.: American Psychological Association.

III. Sample Letter of Agreement for an Organizational Setting

LETTER OF AGREEMENT

Developing the Vision for

(Company Name)

TURNING POINT NORTHWEST
Phone: (425) 985-9244
Fax: (425) 614-1706
www.TurningPointNW.com

Sample only. Consult your own attorney for legal advice.

TURNING POINT NORTHWEST
Kirkland, WA 98006
Phone: 425-985-9244 • E-mail: skleduc@TurningPointNW.com

Date

Dear (Client's Name):

The opportunity to assist (Company Name) with the development of your five-year vision is exciting. I look forward to working with you and the Executive Team.

As we discussed on Friday, the purpose of our work together is to create a compelling vision that will be understood and embraced. Through the development of (Company Name)'s vision, your staff, customers, suppliers, and distributors will feel even more connected to the company and to the outstanding products and services you deliver.

In our time together we will discuss the independent thoughts of the leadership team, explore what will constitute a compelling vision, tie the vision to the values held within (Company Name), and strive to come to mutual agreement. In addition, for six months following the initial visioning session, we will meet monthly for team coaching to maintain momentum.

This letter will serve to document our agreement for Turning Point Northwest to provide this assistance.

The remainder of this letter is organized as follows:

- Background and Objectives
- Proposed Program
- Session Fees
- Contract Terms

After reviewing this letter of agreement, please sign the last page and return the original to me. Of course, if you have any questions please don't hesitate to call me at (phone number).

Best Regards,

Background & Objectives

As organizations grow and mature, the vision that initially provided the means for guiding success may need to be reviewed and redesigned. As well, senior management must present itself as fully aligned, both within the organization to staff members and outside to its customers and suppliers. Time spent in evaluating past successes and proactively anticipating future success (and challenges) is a worthwhile investment.

The objective of this proposed effort is to develop a senior management vision that will be incorporated as the guiding vision for (Company Name). Creating a vision is a process, and as such, takes time. A first step is to bring the senior management team together for a half-day session designed to create greater awareness of individual personality and communication styles, to explore values, and to create a unified vision.

In order to make this session as meaningful as possible, the senior management team will begin thinking about their individual visions for the company prior to attending the visioning session. To supplement the internal thought process, two assessment instruments will be completed by each senior manager and returned to Turning Point Northwest. The information generated from these assessments will be incorporated into the visioning session.

To help ensure that the vision takes hold, we recommend monthly half-day team coaching sessions. During the session we will build upon the successes from the previous month and develop strategies for resolving any challenges that might impede your progress.

Proposed Program
Initial Half-Day Visioning Session

- Design of session: completion of needs assessment and five to six hours of design time for customization of visioning session
- Self-assessment of one's own behavior, communication, and personality style
- Team Profile
- Delivery of half-day session (four to five hours)
- Follow-up discussion
- All materials: handouts, reports, working materials

Follow-On Coaching for Implementing the Vision

- Monthly half-day meetings for six months with senior management team to discuss successes and setbacks
- Each session will build upon the goals and actions tied to the vision

Visioning Session & Coaching Fees

We appreciate your desire to provide an investment in your company to address the "people elements," especially as you prepare to go to the next stage of business development, and our fee reflects our desire to provide a quality program at an affordable cost. The fee for this program, which includes all materials, is $xxxx for an initial half-day visioning session. This fee is substantially discounted from the customized programs we design and deliver.

The monthly team coaching session, with an agreement for a six-month retainer agreement, is set at a monthly flat fee of $xxxx.

Upon acceptance of the contract, Turning Point Northwest will provide an invoice for half of the fee for the visioning session, which is to be paid prior to delivery of the program. The balance is due upon completion of the session. The visioning session will be delivered on (date). (Company Name) will provide the facility for the session.

Monthly coaching fees are due by the first of each month.

The liability of our firm for any services rendered is limited to the amount of the fee billed for these services.

We would be pleased to offer any additional business coaching or consulting at our standard rate of $XXX/hour.

Additional assessment tools can also be made available to other members of your staff. Prices vary, depending upon the instrument. We can discuss your needs and the most appropriate instruments to meet those needs. Examples of assessment instruments include:

- Behavioral assessment
- Communication styles
- Values analysis
- Motivation assessment
- Sales style analysis
- Work environment and employee selection
- Emotional Intelligence assessment

Should you have any questions concerning our approach or plans, please contact (name) at (phone number). If you agree with the proposed outline and would like to proceed, please sign and return the proposal. In turn, I'll sign and return a copy to you. We look forward to working with you on this important initiative.

Best regards,

AGREEMENT FOR A VISIONING AND COACHING PROGRAM

I agree to the proposed outline for a half-day visioning and six months of executive team coaching for (Company Name) as outlined in this proposal.

Accepted for (Company Name) by:

_____   _____
(Client)   Date
President
(Company Name)

Accepted for Turning Point Northwest by:

_____   _____
Sylva Leduc, M.Ed., MPEC   Date
President
TurningPoint Northwest

IV. Values Clarification Exercise

Name _____ Date _____

Clarifying your values for this stage of your life can aid you in shaping your purpose and vision.

In this stage of life or transition, what values are most important to you? What are the values you must honor to be true to this chapter of your life?

First, choose the 10-15 values from the following list that you feel are most important at this time and group them together in strings.

Example: Collaboration/Community/Full self-expression

Second, identify your three or four most important values for this chapter of your life.

_____   _____   _____   _____

Accuracy	Family happiness	Orderliness
Achievement	Focus	Participation
Acknowledgment	Forward the action	Partnership
Advancement	Freedom	Peace
Adventure	Free spirit	Performance
Aesthetics	Free time	Personal power
Affection	Friendship	Pleasure
Authenticity	Growth	Power
Autonomy	Harmony	Precision
Beauty	Health	Productivity
Caring	Help others	Recognition
Challenge	Help society	ResponsibilityRisk-taking
Change	Honesty	Romance
Collaboration	Humor	Self-expression
Community	Independence	Service
Competition	Integrity	Spirituality
Comradeship	Intellectual status	Stability
Connectedness	Joy	Success
Contribution	Knowledge	Time freedom
Creativity	Lack of pretense	Tradition
Directness	Leadership	Trust
Economic security	Leisure	Vitality
Elegance	Lightness	Wealth
Empowerment	Location	Wisdom
Excellence	Loyalty	Zest
Excitement	Nurturing	Add your own: _____

V. Ready to be Coached?

Name: _____

This questionnaire is designed to help you self-assess your readiness for a coaching relationship.

Please circle Yes or No to each question:

1. I will keep appointments with myself to work on my coaching homework.
    Yes   No

2. There is something I want to work on or achieve which I will focus on in my coaching.
    Yes   No

3. I am willing to stop or change behaviors that are interfering with my progress.
    Yes   No

4. I am willing to try new approaches to help me achieve my goals.
    Yes   No

5. Coaching is an appropriate approach to help me accomplish my goals, as opposed to therapy for an emotional issue, consulting for specific problem solving, or specific teaching.
    Yes   No

6. I will take regular actions to help achieve my coaching goals even if I don't see immediate results.
    Yes   No

7. I will be open with my coach about what I like or don't like about how the coaching is going.
    Yes   No

8. I will work collaboratively with my coach to design goals and action steps to move forward.
    Yes   No

VI. Coaching Notes Form

Name _____ Session #_____ Date _____

Current Concerns _____

_____

_____

Past Actions _____

_____

_____

Goals _____

_____

_____

Challenges _____

_____

_____

Action Plans _____

_____

_____

Homework _____

_____

_____

My thoughts _____

_____

_____

VII. Excerpts of the APA Statement on Services by Telephone, Teleconferencing and Internet.

You may view the full version of this document at http://www.apa.org/ethics.

The Ethics Code is not specific with regard to telephone therapy or teleconferencing or any electronically provided services as such and has no rules prohibiting such services. Complaints regarding such matters would be addressed on a case by case basis.

Delivery of services by such media as telephone, teleconferencing and internet is a rapidly evolving area. This will be the subject of APA task forces and will be considered in future revision of the Ethics Code. Until such time as a more definitive judgment is available, the Ethics Committee recommends that psychologists follow Standard 1.04c, Boundaries of Competence, which indicates that "in those emerging areas in which generally recognized standards for preparatory training do not yet exist, psychologists nevertheless take reasonable steps to ensure the competence of their work and to protect patients, clients, students, research participants, and others from harm." Other relevant standards include Assessment (Standards 2.01 -2.10), Therapy (4.01 - 4.09, especially 4.01 Structuring the Relationship and 4.02 Informed Consent to Therapy), and Confidentiality (5.01 - 5.11). Within the General Standards section, standards with particular relevance are 1.03, Professional and Scientific Relationship; 1.04 (a, b, and c), Boundaries of Competence; 1.06, Basis for Scientific and Professional Judgments; 1.07a, Describing the Nature and Results of Psychological Services; 1.14, Avoiding Harm; and 1.25, Fees and Financial Arrangements. Standards under Advertising, particularly 3.01 - 3.03 are also relevant.

Psychologists considering such services must review the characteristics of the services, the service delivery method, and the provisions for confidentiality. Psychologists must then consider the relevant ethical standards and other requirements, such as licensure board rules.

VIII. Sample Coaching Questions

Here are "inquiry" style coaching questions. Use this list to help you think of the type of questions that may be helpful to your clients. Some questions could be answered during the coaching session, and some would best be posed as a homework assignment.

• What has been the most meaningful experience you've had? Please describe what made it so important for you.

• What makes you light up inside?

• What is your biggest passion in this chapter of your life?

• What do co-workers/colleagues think are your biggest strengths?

• What's your sense of purpose?

• What would you like to do to reinforce your plan?

• What gets in your way? What is the most practical thing you can do this week to get around that obstacle?

• What does the mission statement say about this? (when working with organizations)

• How would you prioritize your steps?

• What is the next step?

• How will you know you are making progress?

• Where would you like to see yourself in two years?

• What is most important to you in your work environment?

• What would you consider your most valuable skills?

• If you could change something about yourself, what would you change?

• How do you invest your time? What changes would you like to make in regards to the way you use your time?

• What do you do for pleasure?

• What are you passionate about?

- What would you be willing to give up to reach your goal?

- What do you like best about being a man/woman?

- What qualities do people admire in you?

- What are two things that have been bothering you that you are willing to change?

- If money were no object, how would you spend a week?

- What brings you joy?

- How do you spend your free time? What are your hobbies?

- What energizes you? Turns you off? What feeds you?

- What is the most special vacation you've been on?

- What pursuits have been the most rewarding?

- If you were dying, what would be important to you?

- What is your vision for your emerging life chapter?

- What would you like to do differently?

- What is meaningful to you?

- What strengths do you appreciate about yourself?

- Where would you like to be in five years?

- What is your vision of yourself during retirement?

- What do you want to remember when you're 90?

- What do you consider your gifts?

- How do you define success?

- What would you be willing to give up to reach that goal?

- How did you get to your goal?

- What has been your best achievement?

• What tends to get in your way?

• What time would be more perfect than now?

• What are you passionate about in your current job?

• How do you identify yourself?

• What is an activity/area you want to spend more time in?

• What is an activity/area you'd like to spend less time in?

• What's your most important life dream?

• What would you like to accomplish through our work together?

• What do you think you can do to relate better to others?

• What would you be willing to do to meet your goal?

• What do you see as your most developed strengths?

• In what areas do you feel you want growth?

• What stops you from knowing what to do next?

• What are you tolerating by not doing that?

• What did you like to do as a kid?

• What are your secret passions?

• What do you do to nurture yourself?

• What fulfills you?

• What kind of people do you enjoy being around?

• Where in your life do you feel out of balance?

• What can you do specifically to support that goal?

• What are three wishes you'd like a genie to grant?

- What are you willing to do this week to get out of the box?

- What keeps you from following through?

- What is your biggest fear?

- What is engaging about you?

- What would other people say are your strengths?

- What would you want people to say about you at your funeral?

- What is fun for you?

- How do you want your life to look one year from now?

- If you had six months to live, how would you spend the time? What could you do to do that now?

- How are you going to implement what you learn in this session?

- What is a worthwhile tradeoff to get what you want?

- What are you willing to do to get what you want?

- On a scale of one to ten, how motivated are you to accomplish that goal?

- How much do you want to be a success?

- What is your biggest fear about getting what you want?

- Who is your role model and why?

- What skills do you have right now that will help you get what you want?

- What are your three most important values?

- What do you think your mission is?

- What do you want others to say about you on your 100th birthday?

- What do you want to accomplish before dying?

- If money or fear were not considerations, what would you do with your life?

- What keeps you awake at night?

- What surprises you about yourself?

- What one problem in the world would you solve if you could?

- If you couldn't fail, what would you do?

- What are you tolerating now in your life?

- What do you spend your money/time on?

- What do you think is your purpose in life?

- What matters most to you?

- Which unhelpful habit would you eliminate?

- What do you do well?

- What are you good at that no one notices?

- What are some unusual things about you?

- When coaching is over, how will you know it was successful?

Notes

CHAPTER 1: THE PATH FROM THERAPIST TO COACH

1. I am appreciative of Rich Fettke, MCC for this historical background: This definition of coaching came from the Professional & Personal Coaches Association (PPCA). It was first published in 1997 on the PPCA website and in the PPCA's media packet. The definition was created by a group of PPCA member volunteers and several board members who also interviewed several top coaches and coach training organizations. The PPCA and the ICF merged in 1998. The PPCA had a large dues-paying membership and a full set of industry ethics and standards. The ICF had incredible media exposure and a large email database. Bringing the two groups together created a synergistic effect for the coaching field.

2. Whitworth, L., Kimsey-House, H., & Sandahl, P. (1998). *Co-active coaching: New skills for coaching people toward success in work and life.* Palo Alto, CA: Davies-Black.

3. Gallwey, T. W. (1997). *The inner game of tennis.* Random House.

4. Hudson, F. M. (1999). *The handbook of coaching: A comprehensive resource guide for managers, executives, consultants, and human resource professionals.* San Francisco: Jossey-Bass.

5. Crane, T. G. (1998). *The heart of coaching: Using transformational coaching to create a high-performance culture.* San Diego: FTA Press.

6. Adapted from the International Coach Federation's White Paper: The nature and scope of coaching (2000). For additional information contact the International Coach Federation at www.coachfederation.org.

7. Richardson, C. (1998). *Take time for your life: A personal coach's seven-step program for creating the life you want.* New York: Bantam Doubleday Dell Publishing.

8. Gennep, A. V. (1908). The rites of passage. Chicago: University of Chicago Press.

9. Levinson, D. J. (1973). *The seasons of a man's life.* New York: Knopf.

10. Levinson, D. J. (1996). *The seasons of a woman's life.* New York: Knopf.

11. See Note 4.

12. Hudson, F. M. (1999). The adult years: Mastering the art of self-renewal (Rev. ed.). San Francisco: Jossey-Bass.

13. Hall, D. T., Otazo, K. L., & Hollenbeck, G. P. (1999). Behind the closed doors: What really happens in executive coaching. *Organizational Dynamics, 27*(3), 39-53.

14. Drucker, P. F. (1996). *The effective executive*. New York: HarperCollins.

15. Diedrich, R. (1996). An iterative approach to executive coaching. *Consulting Psychology Journal: Practice and Research, 48*(2), 61-66.

16. Adapted from R. Hargrove, (2000). *Masterful coaching fieldbook*. San Francisco: Jossey-Bass/Pfeiffer.

17. Sappington, A. (1988). *Adjustment: Theory, Research, and Personal Applications*. Pacific Grove, CA: Brooks/Cole.

18. Jung, C. (1958). *The undiscovered self*. New York: Little, Brown.

19. Schultz, D. P. (1977) *Growth psychology: Models of the Healthy Personality*. New York: Van Nostrand Reinhold.

20. Frankl, V. E. (1962). *Man's search for meaning: An introduction to logotherapy*. Boston: Beacon Press.

21. Maslow, A. H. (1968). *Toward a psychology of being* (2nd ed.). New York: Van Nostrand Reinhold.

22. Maslow, A. H. (1955). Deficiency motivation and growth motivation. In M. R. Jones (Ed.), *Nebraska Symposium on Motivation*. Lincoln: University of Nebraska Press.

23. Rogers, C. R. (1959). A theory of therapy, personality, and interpersonal relationships, as developed In the client-centered framework. In S. Koch (Ed.), *Psychology: The study of a science* (Vol. 3). New York: McGraw-Hill.

24. Rogers, C. R., & Dymond, R. (Eds.) (1954). *Psychotherapy and personality change*. Chicago: University of Chicago Press.

CHAPTER 2:
COACHING PHILOSOPHY AND THE CAAACS MODEL OF COACHING

1. Whitworth, L., Kimsey-House, H., & Sandahl, P. (1998). *Co-active coaching: New skills for coaching people toward success in work and life*. Palo Alto, CA : Davies-Black, 1998.

2. Kolb, D. A., & Boyatzis, R. E. (1970). Goal-setting and self-directed behavior change. *Human Relations, 23*(5), 439-457.

3. Specht, L., & Sandlin, P. (1991). The differential effects of experiential learning activities and traditional lecture classes in accounting. *Simulations and Gaming, 22*(2), 196-210.

4. Argyris, C., & Schon, D. A. (1974). *Theory in practice: Increasing professional effectiveness.* San Francisco: Jossey-Bass.

5. Hargrove, R. (1995). *Masterful coaching: Extraordinary results by impacting people and the way they think and work together.* San Francisco: Jossey-Bass/Pfeiffer.

6. See Note 5.

7. Whitworth and others. *Co-active coaching.* See Note 1.

8. Hudson, F. M. (1999). *The handbook of coaching: A comprehensive resource guide for managers, executives, consultants, and human resource professionals.* San Francisco: Jossey-Bass.

CHAPTER 3: ETHICAL AND LEGAL ISSUES IN COACHING

1. Jeffrey E. Barnett, Psy.D. is a licensed psychologist who publishes actively on ethics and legal issues in mental health. He is a past-president of the Maryland Psychological Association and is that organization's representative on the Council of Representatives of the American Psychological Association. He is also the president-elect of the APA's Division of State and Provincial Psychological Association Affairs. Dr. Barnett is a member of the Board of Directors of APA's Division of Independent Practice. O. Brandt Caudill, Jr. Esq., of Callahan, McCune & Willis, LLP, presents and publishes widely in the areas of ethics and legal issues in the mental health field.

2. Bonnie R. Benitez, Esq. is General Counsel and Zachary Pelchat, Esq. is Legislative Counsel for the California Association of Marriage and Family Therapists.

3. Caudill, O. B. Personal communication. July 21, 2001.

4. Caudill, O. B. Personal communication. July 21, 2001.

5. Barnett, J. E. (May, 2000). Yes, but is it ethical? *42 Online*, the online journal of the Division of Independent Practice, American Psychological Association. Journal available for members at http://www.division42.org.

6. Benitez, B. R., and Pelchat, Z. Personal communication. May 5, 2001.

7. For more information about the International Coach Federation, see its website, www.coachfederation.org. For more information about the Professional Coaches and Mentors Association, go to www.pcmaonline.com.

8. The *Independent Practitioner* can be found at the American Psychological Association's Division 42 website, www.div42.org.

9. Caudill, O. B. Personal communication. July 21, 2001.

10. Barnett, J. E. Personal communication. July 21, 2001.

11. Benitez, B. R., and Pelchat, Z. Personal communication. May 5, 2001.

12. Barnett, J. E. (May, 2000). Yes, but is it ethical? See Note 5.

13. Barnett, J. E. Personal communication. July 21, 2001.

14. See Note 13.

15. See the Appendix to view a sample agreement form. Also, Richard R. Kilburg has provided a less legalistic model agreement for coaching services in Kilburg, R. R. (2000). *Executive coaching: Developing managerial wisdom in a world of chaos.* Washington, D.C.: American Psychological Association.

16. Barnett, J. E. Personal communication. July 21, 2001.

17. Benitez, B. R., and Pelchat, Z. Personal communication. May 5, 2001.

18. See the Appendix for excerpts of the *APA Statement on Services by Telephone, Teleconferencing and Internet.* View the full version of this document at http://www.apa.org/ethics.

CHAPTER 4: INITIAL PROCESS

1. Witherspoon, R. (2000). Starting smart: Clarifying coaching goals and roles. In *Coaching for leadership,* edited by Goldsmith, M., Lyons, L. and Freas, A. San Francisco: Jossey-Bass. Also see: Witherspoon, R. & White, R. (1998). *Four essential ways that coaching can help executives.* Greensborough, North Carolina: Center for Creative Leadership.

CHAPTER 5: DEVELOPING THE COACHING ALLIANCE

1. Flaherty, J. (1999). *Coaching: Evoking excellence in others.* Boston: Butterworth-Heinemann.

2. Perls, F. S. (1973). *The Gestalt approach and eye witness to therapy.* Ben Lomond, CA: Science and Behavior Books.

3. Specht, L., & Sandlin, P. (1991). The differential effects of experiential learning activities and traditional lecture classes in accounting. *Simulations and Gaming, 22*(2), 196-210.

4. Hargrove, R. (2000) *Masterful coaching fieldbook.* San Francisco: Jossey-Bass.

CHAPTER 6: COACHING TECHNIQUES

1. Adapted from R. Hargrove (2000), *Masterful coaching fieldbook.* San Francisco: Jossey-Bass.

2. Flaherty, J. (1999). *Coaching: Evoking excellence in others.* Boston: Butterworth-Heinemann.

3. Hargrove, R. (1995). *Masterful coaching: Extraordinary results by impacting people and the way they think and work together.* San Francisco: Jossey-Bass/Pfeiffer.

4. Hargrove, R. (2000). See Note 1.

5. Whitworth, L., Kimsey-House, H., & Sandahl, P. (1998). *Co-active coaching.* Palo Alto, CA: Davies-Black Publishing.

6. Cooperrider, D. L., Sorensen, Jr., P. F., Whitney, D., Yaeger, T. F. (Eds.) (2000). *Appreciative inquiry: Rethinking human organization toward a positive theory of change.* Champaign, IL: Stipes Publishing, L.L.C.

7. Hammond, S. (1998). *The thin book of appreciative inquiry.* Plano, TX: Thin Book Publishing Company.

8. Hammond, S. (1998). See Note 7.

9. Raths, L., Merrill, H., & Sidney, S. (1968). *Values and teaching: Working with values in the classroom.* Columbus, OH: Charles E. Merrill.

10. Murphy, J. S., & Hudson, F. M. (1995). *The joy of old: A guide to successful elderhood.* Altadena, CA: Geode Press.

11. Hudson, F. M. (1999). *The adult years: Mastering the art of self-renewal* (rev. ed.). San Francisco: Jossey-Bass.

12. Hudson, F. M. (1999). *The handbook of coaching: A comprehensive resource guide for managers, executives, consultants, and human resource professionals.* San Francisco: Jossey-Bass.

13. Richardson, C. (1998). *Take time for your life: A personal coach's seven-step program for creating the life you want.* New York: Broadway Books.

14. Leonard, T. J., & Laursen, B. (1998). *The portable coach: Twenty-eight surefire strategies for business and personal success.* New York: Scribner.

15. Rossi, E. L. (1991). *The twenty-minute break: Reduce stress, maximize performance, and improve health and emotional well-being using the new science of ultradian rhythms.* Los Angeles: J. P. Tarcher.

16. Erickson, M. (1989). *The collected papers of Milton H. Erickson on hypnosis* (Vols. I-IV). Rossi, E. L. (Ed.). New York: Irvington Publishers.

17. EMDR is an acronym for Eye Movement Desensitization and Reprocessing, a clinical treatment that integrates many of the successful elements of a range of therapeutic approaches in combination with eye movements or other forms of rhythmical stimulation in ways that stimulate the brain's information processing system. For more information on how Sandra Foster and colleague Jennifer Lendl integrated

EMDR into coaching, see Foster, S. & Lendl, J. (1996). Eye Movement Desensitization and Reprocessing: Four case studies of a new tool for executive coaching and restoring employee performance after setbacks. *Consulting Psychology Journal 48,* 155-161.

18. Hall, D. T., Otazo, K. L., & Hollenbeck, G. P. (1999). Behind the closed doors: What really happens in executive coaching. *Organizational Dynamics, 27*(3), 39-53.

19. Whitworth and colleagues (1998). *Co-active coaching.*

20. Argyris, C. (1990). *Overcoming organizational defenses: Facilitating organizational learning.* Needham, MA: Allyn & Bacon.

21. Nadler, R. S. and Luckner, J. L. *Processing the experience: Strategies to enhance and generalize learning.* 2nd Ed. Dubuque, Iowa: Kendall/Hunt Publishing.

22. Whitworth and colleagues (1998). See Note 5.

23. Adapted from F. M. Hudson (1999). See Note 12.

24. Whitworth and colleagues (1998). See Note 5.

CHAPTER 7: ASSESSMENT IN COACHING

1. Isachsen, O. (1996). *Joining the entrepreneurial elite: Four styles to business success.* Palo Alto, CA: Davies-Black Publishing.

2. The MBTI, CPI, and FIRO-B instruments are available through Consulting Psychologists Press (www.cpp-db.com). Online administration of these instruments is available on a subscription basis as a benefit for students and alumni of the College of Executive Coaching certification. Online administration avoids the potential ethical liability of mailing sensitive testing instruments to distant clients.

3. Isachsen, O., & Berens, L. V., (1988). *Working together: A personality-centered approach to management.* Coronado, CA: Neworld Management Press.

4. Information about the Benchmarks tool and the Campbell Leadership Index tool is available at the website of the Center for Creative Leadership, at www.ccl.org. For an overview of assessment tools, see K. E. Morical (1999), A product review: 360 assessments, in *Training and Development, 4,* 43-47.

5. Sederburg, M. & Rogelberg, S. (1998). 360 degree feedback: Methodological advice from multiple sources. *The Industrial and Organizational Psychologist, 36*(2), 10.

CHAPTER 8: COACHING TRANSITIONS AND FACILITATING STRATEGIC LIFE PLANS

1. Jung, C. (1958). *The undiscovered self.* New York: Little, Brown.

2. Hudson, F. M. (1999). *The adult years: Mastering the art of self-renewal* (Rev. ed.). San Francisco: Jossey-Bass.

3. Bridges, W. (1980). (2nd Ed.). *Transitions: Making sense of life's changes.* Reading, MA: Addison-Wesley.

4. Bolles, R. N. (2000) *What color is your parachute? 2001 edition: A practical manual for job-hunters and career-changers.* (1983 Ed., revised and enlarged). Berkeley, CA: Ten Speed Press.

5. The Myers-Briggs Type Indicator, Strong Interest Inventory, and MBTI Career Report are available through Consulting Psychologists Press (www.cpp-db.com). Online administration of these instruments is available on a subscription basis as a benefit for students and alumni of the College of Executive Coaching certification program.

6. See Note 5.

7. Isachsen, O. (1996). *Joining the entrepreneurial elite: Four styles to business success.* Palo Alto, CA: Davies-Black Publishing.

8. Hudson, F. M., & McLean, P. D. (1995). *Life launch: A passionate guide to the rest of your life.* Santa Barbara, CA: Hudson Institute Press.

CHAPTER 9: EXECUTIVE COACHING AND LEADERSHIP

1. Bennis, W. (1994). *On becoming a leader.* Reading, MA: Perseus Books.

2. Covey, S. (1989) *The seven habits of highly effective people: Restoring the character ethic.* New York: Simon & Schuster.

3. Covey, S. (1991). *Principle-centered leadership.* New York: Summit Books.

4. Information on the FranklinCovey organization is found at http://www.franklincovey.com.

5. Bennis (1994). See Note 1.

6. Bennis, W. & Nanus, B. (1997) *Leaders: Strategies for taking charge.* New York: HarperBusiness.

7. Kouzes, J. M., & Posner, B. Z. (1985). *The leadership challenge: How to keep getting extraordinary things done in organizations.* San Francisco: Jossey-Bass.

8. Kouzes, J. M., & Posner, B. Z. (1987). *The leadership challenge planner: An action guide to achieving your personal best.* San Francisco: Jossey-Bass/Pfeiffer.

9. The Center for Creative Leadership website is http://www.ccl.org.

10. Bennis, W. (1994). *On becoming a leader.* Reading, MA: Perseus Books.

11. Pearman, R. R. (1998). *Hard wired leadership: Unleashing the power of personality to become a new millennium leader.* Palo Alto, CA: Davies-Black.

12. See Note 11.

13. Goleman, D. (1998). *Working with emotional intelligence.* New York: Bantam Books.

14. Adapted from R. Hargrove (2000). *Masterful coaching fieldbook.* San Francisco: Jossey-Bass.

15. Hersey, P., Blanchard, K. H., & Johnson, D. E. (1996). *Management of organizational behavior: Utilizing human resources* (7th Ed.). Upper Saddle River: Prentice Hall.

16. Blanchard, K. H., & Johnson, S. (1982). *The one minute manager®.* New York: Morrow.

17. Blanchard, K. H., Zigarmi, P., & Zigarmi, D. (1985). *Leadership and the one minute manager®.* New York: Morrow.

18. Kanter, R. M. (1999). The enduring skills of change leaders. In the Peter F. Drucker Foundation's *Leader to Leader* series, No. 13, Summer (http://drucker.org/leaderbooks/l2l/summer99/kanter.html).

19. Senge, P. M. (1990). *The fifth discipline: The art and practice of the learning organization.* New York: Doubleday/Currency, xiv-xv.

CHAPTER 10: EMOTIONAL INTELLIGENCE AND COACHING

1. Goleman, D. (1995). *Emotional intelligence.* New York: Bantam Books.

2. Goleman, D. (1998). *Working with emotional intelligence.* New York: Bantam Books.

3. Gardner, H. (1983). *The theory of multiple intelligences.* New York: Basic Books.

4. Boyatzis, R., Goleman, D., and Rhee, K. (2000). In R. Bar-On & J. D. A. Parker, Eds., *The handbook of emotional intelligence: Theory, development, assessment, and application at home, school, and in the workplace.* San Francisco: Jossey-Bass.

5. Bar-On, R. (1998). BarOn Emotional Quotient Inventory. Toronto: Multi-Health Systems.

6. Salovey, P., & Mayer, J. D. (1990). Emotional intelligence. *Imagination, Cognition, and Personality, 9,* 185-211.

7. Table 1 is adapted from Boyatzis, R., Goleman, D., and Rhee, K. (2000). See Note 4.

8. An unpublished study attributed to Burckle, M. and Boyatzis, R. (1999) in *ECI accreditation training: Driving personal and professional development training materials.* (2001). Boston: Hay/McBer Training Resources Group.

9. Arnold, K. (1995). *Lives of promise: What becomes of high school valedictorians: A fourteen-year study of achievement and life choices.* San Francisco: Jossey-Bass.

10. Vaillant, G. (1977). *Adaptation to life.* Boston: Little, Brown.

11. Goleman, D. (1998). *Working with emotional intelligence.* See Note 2.

12. Seligman, M. E. P. (1998). *Learned optimism: How to change your mind and your life.* New York: Pocket Books.

13. McClelland, D. (1998). Identifying competencies with behavioral-event interviews. *Psychological Science, 9*(5), 331-339.

14. Jones, C. (1986). *Programming productivity.* New York: McGraw-Hill.

15. Table 2 is adapted from R. Bar-On (1970), *Proceedings of the 105th American Psychological Association.*

16. The Multifactor Emotional Intelligence Scale (MEIS™) is available through Charles J. Wolfe Associates in Connecticut.

17. Mayer, J., Caruso, D., & Salovey, P. (2000). Selecting a measure of emotional intelligence: The case for ability scales. In R. Bar-On & J. D. A. Parker (Eds.), *The handbook of emotional intelligence.* New York: Jossey-Bass.

18. The EQ Map is available through Q-Metrics in San Francisco.

19. Feldman, D. (1999). *The handbook of emotionally intelligent leadership: Inspiring others to achieve results.* Falls Church, VA: Leadership Performance Solutions.

20. See Note 19.

21. For a detailed expanded description of twenty-two best-practice guidelines for developing emotional intelligence programs, see the technical report by Cherniss, C., Emmerling, R., Cowan, K., & Adler, M. (1998), issued by the Consortium for Research on Emotional Intelligence in Organizations: (http://eiconsortium.org/research/technical_report.htm).

22. For more information about the Emotional Competence Training Program, see the web site of the Consortium for Research on Emotional Intelligence in Organizations: (http://eiconsortium.org/model_programs/emotional_competence_training.htm).

CHAPTER 11: COACHING FOR PERSONAL AND PROFESSIONAL DEVELOPMENT

1. Drucker, P. (1993). *The effective executive.* New York: HarperCollins.

2. Moxley, R. S., & Wilson, P. O. (1998). A systems approach to leadership development. In McCauley, C. D., Moxley, R. S., & Velsor, E. V. (Eds.) *The handbook of leadership development.* San Francisco: Jossey-Bass.

Jeffrey E. Barnett, Psy.D.
barnetthome@erols.com

Bonnie R. Benitez, Esq.
www.camft.org

Paul Best, Ph.D., MPEC and Eileen Sunzeri, M.S.
pbest@targetmanagement.com
eileensun@targetmanagement.com

O. Brandt Caudill, Esq.
bcaudill@cmwlaw.net

Judi Craig, Ph.D., MCC
judi@coachsquared.com

Barbara Doyle, M.A.
midlifevision@aol.com

Sandra Foster, Ph.D., MPEC
samrolf@aol.com

Sylva Leduc, M.Ed., MPEC
skleduc@TurningPointNW.com

Christine Brown McCarthy, MBA, MSW
christinemccarthy@home.com

Ana Maria Montes, Ph.D., MPEC
ana@executivecoachcollege.com

Relly Nadler, Psy.D., MPEC
rnadler@truenorthleadership.com

Zachary Pelchat, Esq.
www.camft.org

Marcia Reynolds, M.A., M.Ed., MCC
covisioner@aol.com

Edward H. Rockey, Ph.D., MPEC
erockey@pepperdine.edu

Robert J. Voyle, Psy.D. MPEC
rob@voyle.com

ABOUT THE AUTHOR

Jeffrey E. Auerbach, Ph.D., MPEC, is the founder and president of the College of Executive Coaching. Dr. Auerbach is a certified Master Personal and Executive Coach and an International Coach Federation Chapter President. He is also a licensed psychologist and a licensed marriage and family therapist. He closed his clinical practice years ago and made the complete transition to personal and executive coaching. Dr. Auerbach has trained thousands of mental health professionals in coaching methodology. He travels widely to speak, lead workshops and coach entrepreneurs, executives and organizations. He also maintains a thriving telephone-based coaching practice.

For more information on his services, contact:

College of Executive Coaching
3875 Telegraph Road A PMB 115
Ventura, CA 93003
Telephone: (805) 647-7760
Fax: (805) 647-7660
Email: training@executivecoachcollege.com
www.executivecoachcollege.com

Master Personal and Executive Coach Certification
The College of Executive Coaching

The College of Executive Coaching is the leader in coach training for professionals with graduate degrees. The Master Personal and Executive Coach (MPEC) Certification is a comprehensive program incorporating in-person training and distance learning with an outstanding faculty of ten Ph.D. level professional coaches.

Most of the applicants to the training program are experienced, successful professionals who are motivated by a desire to create positive, meaningful change for their clients and our world. As highly trained professionals they know they can help people achieve their highest goals and they seek to be compensated well for their services.

The Master Personal and Executive Coach Certificate Program (MPEC™) can help you bridge the gap between your desire to transition into an effective, well-compensated career niche and the realization of your goal.

Our diverse faculty provides you with a variety of role models and coaching styles to help you develop a coaching approach that matches your strengths.

The training program consists of a post-graduate level curriculum to provide you with the coaching and business skills you need to have a highly marketable coaching practice.

Contact Information:

Master Personal and Executive Coach Certification Program
College of Executive Coaching
3875 Telegraph Road A PMB 115 • Ventura, CA 93003
(805) 647-7760 • (805) 647-7660 FAX
www.executivecoachcollege.com
training@executivecoachcollege.com

INFORMATION REQUEST AND ORDER FORM

_____ Please send me more information on the Master Personal and Executive Coach Certification Program

_____ Please send me _____ copies of the book: *Personal and Executive Coaching: The Complete Guide for Mental Health Professionals.*

PLEASE PRINT CLEARLY:

Name _____

Address _____

City _____

State _____ Country_____ Zip _____

Telephone _____Fax _____

E-Mail _____

Payment: ____VISA _____ MasterCard

_____Check (Payable to: Executive College Press)

—— —— —— ——   —— —— —— ——   —— —— —— ——   —— —— —— ——

Expiration Date of Card _____/_____

Books _____ x $39.95 (U.S.) ($51.95 Canada)

Tax _____ (CA residents only add 8%)

Shipping _____ (U.S.- $4.00 for one book; $2.50 for each additional book)
(International - $9.00 U.S. for the first book, $5.00 for each additional book)

Total $ _____

Normal delivery time in the U.S.A. is 4 -5 days.

College of Executive Coaching

3875 Telegraph Road A PMB 115 • Ventura, CA 93003

(805) 647-7760 • (805) 647-7660 FAX

www.executivecoachcollege.com • training@executivecoachcollege.com